SYLVIA ST.CYR

LOVE
VS.
FEAR

CONQUER YOUR FEARS BY TRUSTING
IN GOD'S INCREDIBLE LOVE FOR YOU

LOVE VS. FEAR
Copyright © 2017 by Sylvia St.Cyr

ISBN: 978-1-4866-1477-6

Word Alive Press
131 Cordite Road, Winnipeg, MB R3W 1S1
www.wordalivepress.ca

WORD ALIVE
—P R E S S—

Library and Archives Canada Cataloguing in Publication

St. Cyr, Sylvia, author
    Love vs. fear : conquer your fears by trusting in God's incredible love for you / Sylvia St. Cyr.

Issued in print and electronic formats.
ISBN 978-1-4866-1477-6 (softcover).--ISBN 978-1-4866-1478-3 (ebook)

    1. Fear--Religious aspects--Christianity. 2. God (Christianity)--Love. I. Title.

BV4908.5.S7 2017   248.8'6   C2017-903461-8
                                           C2017-903462-6

I would like to dedicate this book to all the girls and women out there who struggle with their identity. You are so loved by our Heavenly Father.

CONTENTS

ACKNOWLEDGEMENTS

It has taken me years to write this book and make all the revisions. I have had some incredible people in my corner pushing me forward, and I would like to take this opportunity to thank them.

Thank you, Mom, for all you've done in my life up until this point. Thank you for always encouraging me to keep shining and giving my best. You used to say that you wanted to become a nurse and then share your nursing talents in Africa. That was before you had a degree in anything. Then, after your boys were done high school, you actually went out and made all of it happen! Your pursuit of your dreams has given me the courage to pursue mine, and I am truly grateful.

The support from my family and my husband's family has meant a lot as I wrote this book.

Thank you to my amazing children, Zevry and Moxie, who have taught me so many life lessons. You are such an incredible part of my life and have also given me a lot of the inspiration that is in the pages to follow.

Amanda Legault. As far as writing this book is concerned, you have always cheered me on to get it done, and also taken my phone calls to hear me cry about certain difficult parts. Thank you for walking this writing journey with me.

Evan Braun. When I knew absolutely nothing about the writing or publishing world, you took me under your wing and gave me priceless information. Thank you for that and also for editing this book!

The Word Alive Press team who has worked with me on this book, and also encouraged me to continue on until it was published. Thank you! Jen, you are not only my boss, but a good friend who is honest and encouraging. Tia, you make me laugh and you are also not afraid to share your opinion and be real with me. Thank you, ladies!

Thank you, Shaun, for all your support. You are my best friend, my husband, the father of our children, and such an incredible man. Thank you for being real, asking tough questions when they needed to be asked, and pushing me on in my hopes and dreams. Your love and support mean the world to me.

And of course, thank you, Lord, for giving me the words to speak and the platform on which to do it. You are such a good Father, Friend, Counsellor, and Support. Without You, life is not possible and the patience You show me, the love You give me every moment, reminds me that I can live a life without fear when I abide in You! May this book be a reflection of Your heart for Your people!

INTRODUCTION

At every turn, fear tries to bully its way into our hearts, to dig its roots in and grow. There are many instances in my life when I've allowed fear to take over. My self-worth has often been left to however I feel that day. Then what would happen? I would screw something up. It could've been small, but the fear in my head would start to attack: *Look at what you've done. Do you think this is good? No! This is stupid. You're stupid. Just walk away and own that you are no good!*

Does this ever happen to you?

It happened even while I was writing this book. Writing was the "easy" part. After that, the voice of fear inside my head grew loud.

Once the book was edited, I noticed a ton of little red marks in it. If I had just looked at my manuscript rationally, I could have told myself, "This is part of the process, so fix what you must and move on. This is making your book better."

But is that where my thoughts went? No. When I looked at the edited version for the first time, I thought, "All these red marks are proof that I'm stupid, that I'm not good enough, that I was foolish to ever think I could write a book! So what did I do? I didn't touch it for months. Just shy of a year, I left it and lived life the way I normally did.

When I did finally gain the courage to sit down and start looking through the edited version, so many months later, I sat in front of my computer and couldn't move. I phoned a friend who had been through the editing process before and asked her if my feelings were normal. Although she listened to me and offered me encouragement, her editing process had been a breeze.

Then I literally cried and hyperventilated for about an hour. All those feelings of worthlessness and stupidity came flooding back. But once I cried all my tears and asked God to walk this road with me, I began to type and revise. I could feel His presence urging me on, letting me know that I was not alone.

How ironic that I was so filled with fear while writing a book on fear. Or perhaps it's actually fitting.

What are you afraid of today? What's holding you back from doing something that you normally love? Do you believe that you can overcome it?

Due to the fact that you're reading these words right now, you can see that I persevered through and overcame my fear. These pages are filled with stories of ordinary people doing extraordinary things, because of a God who pursues them and loves them.

I wrote this book to encourage believers, especially women, who have struggled with believing that they carry any worth or influence in the world around them. In turn, God has encouraged me with the words written, and for that I can take no credit.

People have said that the opposite of love is hate. I believe that love and hate can simply be two sides of the same coin. Both share a care and concern. I believe that the opposite of love is fear. 1 John 4:18 has reiterated that thought in my life. In this book, I share not only my journey on that road, but also the journeys of many other courageous people. People who were not perfect, but said "Yes!" to God and have seen miracles happen because of it.

This book is not a five-step program to permanently get rid of all the fear in your life. However, it offers the real-life scenarios of people who felt crushed or less than enough, and allows you to see how God can turn those situations around for His glory! With God, all things are possible.

My hope and prayer is that this book will offer light and hope into situations that otherwise look dark and dismal.

CHAPTER ONE

HUMAN NATURE

I am thankful to God for the freedom that comes through our Lord Jesus, the Anointed One! So on the one hand, I devotedly serve God's law with my mind; but on the other hand, with my flesh, I serve the principle of sin.

—Romans 7:25 (The Voice)

FEAR. JUST A PART OF LIFE. SOMETHING WE BATTLE AND SUCCUMB TO every day, from giving a speech at your best friend's wedding to climbing the ladder to put up Christmas lights on the house. Some fears we overcome, and others we allow to dominate our lives. Do we have any control over these fears? Are we destined to live by the way they make us feel? Or is there a better way?

Yes, there is a better way. Fear does *not* have to overtake our lives.

Although we all deal with fear in some aspect, fear cannot rule us without our permission. Fear is not like an arm or a leg. It doesn't grow without our consent. Fear is an outside force that tries to live inside us and control our every move. The truth is that fear has no power except that which we give it.

You may be thinking, *That's easy for you to say, as you've probably never had a phobia or a body-controlling, sweat-dripping grip-of-fear attack.* Well, I actually do have many fears. It is human nature to fear something, anything. But when those fears approach, we have options. We are not fated to stay in bondage to fear's grip. Will fear ever leave us alone? No. It is relentless, but we can gain the tools we need to overcome this monster and gain our lives back! Sound good? Then keep reading.

LEARNED FEARS

The day we're born, we naturally have in us two fears: the fear of falling and the fear of loud noises. All other fears are learned.

Take a second and think about that. Consider any fear you have that's not of falling or loud noises—like spiders, for example. That was learned! How about speaking in public? That was learned. The fear of death? Drowning? Going to jail? All learned! Wikipedia tells us, "People develop specific fears as a result of learning."[1]

Who did we learn this from? As awesome as our parents may be, or not, we learned a great deal from them, including some of their fears.

We may have also learned it from our siblings. I had the privilege of growing up with three older brothers. I will never forget an experience I had when I was seven years old. I was about to go to the dentist to get some cavities filled. My brothers knew this and did what big brothers do very well—they proceeded to tell me all about the massive needle ("An as-big-as-my-arm kind of massive needle") that the dentist was going to stab into my gums before he drilled and hacked at my teeth. Sound effects were included.

I was not scared of the dentist before; I had been to the dentist prior. Needless to say, after this story from my oh-so-wise brothers, I surely was!

We also learn from our peers. As children, and even teens, we are very susceptible to the environment around us. Peer pressure is a real thing, even going into the workforce!

As a child, I remember my dad finishing every day off by watching the eleven o'clock news. The few times I watched with him, it left me feeling terribly afraid. Afraid that the world was in rough shape, that we could all die very soon. I'm not saying the news was bad. How could I, as a journalist for my local newspaper? But as a child, the news seemed to focus only on the terrible events occurring in the world around us. Who broke into what house? How many people died in this earthquake? How many people were held captive in that war-torn country?

That's why I do not watch the news.

---

1   *Wikipedia*, "Fear." Date of access: September 4, 2016 (www.wikipedia.org/wiki/fear).

Whoever we have learned our fears from—our parents, siblings, peers, co-workers, the government, or the news—they were learned and they can be unlearned!

TOP TEN FEARS

People around the world suffer with fear. Whether you live in the remote jungles of Bora Bora or in the fast-paced technological jungle of Japan, people have always come up against fear. Take a second, but only a second, to think about some of your fears. Write what you would consider your top three here:

1. _____

2. _____

3. _____

Are your fears rational? By that I mean, has something happened specifically to you to cause this fear? Or are they irrational in the sense that nothing bad has ever happened to you based on your fear, but the fear is there anyway?

Mine, as I write this book, would have to be (1) the dark, (2) not being liked, and (3) spiders (but only big ones). These have not always been the top three and they will probably change within a year, because that's how fear likes to take over our lives. They constantly change. Also, mine are all irrational. My fear of the dark comes simply from watching too many scary movies as a teen. My fear of not being liked is more of an insecurity than anything. And the spiders? Well. Have I been bitten by a spider and become deathly ill? Not even once. Therefore, irrational.

With some research, I have found that the top ten fears people have all over the world are relatively consistent: From selfhelpcollective.com, it says the top 10 fears are as follows.

Flying
Public speaking
Heights
The dark
Intimacy
Death
Failure
Rejection
Spiders/Snakes/Rats
Commitment[2]

It's so interesting to me that death is number six! Think about it. Well, actually, that's the problem. Most fears are in our minds, but if you think about it, what is the worst thing that could happen? Well, I would think it would be death, yet there are things we fear even worse than the worst.

Looking closer at my fears has brought me more clarity as well. I say that because I'm not actually afraid of the dark; I'm actually afraid of the unknown, of someone or something that I cannot see. When I go to bed without my husband beside me, whether he is still up or somewhere else for the evening, I find it incredibly hard to sleep. What thoughts run through my head? Well, maybe that someone will come into my home and hurt me or my kids.

Now, is this a rational fear? Not really. I have been alive for thirty years, and when I think about it, has this *ever* happened to me? No. Has it happened to anyone close to me? No. It has happened to a friend of a friend. Even then, it got resolved just fine.

I think that because it happened once, it will happen to me. Logical? Rational? Not in the least. What is the probability? Considering that I live in Canada, probably one percent—if that.

Even after thinking it through, the fear doesn't totally fade away. But it's a start. You can do this with any irrational fear you have. Think about the outcome of your fear coming to pass.

---

2   Steve M. Nash, *Self-Help Collective*, "Are These Your Top 10 Fears?" Date of access: September 4, 2016 (http://www.selfhelpcollective.com/top-10-fears.html).

Let's say you're afraid of failure. You don't step out in your career and tell the boss about your great idea because you think maybe he'll hate it. You never even try, because your fear of failure holds you back.

So make it rational. Let's say you tell him your great idea. What happens? Honestly, one of two things. If you tell him and he likes it, well, the sky is the limit! You may get a raise, or your idea could turn into a profit for you. If you tell your boss the idea and he hates it, or simply doesn't like it, then he says no. Are you worse off than before? Well, seeing as it wouldn't have gone anywhere if you didn't tell him and now it still hasn't gone anywhere, you are in the same place, not further behind. See?

HOLDING US BACK

Whatever fear you deal with—whether it's one of the top ten, like flying, taking the elevator, public speaking, or something a little more obscure, like cotton balls—what do all fears have in common? They hold us back in our lives. Would you not agree? They keep us from being all we could be.

> WHAT DO ALL FEARS HAVE IN COMMON? THEY HOLD US BACK IN OUR LIVES

Think about what fear does to your body, physically. Close your eyes for a second and think about your biggest fear. Maybe someone chasing you in the dark, tons of spiders crawling over your body, or standing on the edge of a very tall skyscraper. Are you sweating yet? Your heart racing? Palms clammy? You may even find yourself curling inward, into a ball, instinctively protecting your major organs.

Without thinking about it, our fears control our physical reactions, like our heart rate—and our actions and environment as well. Fear tries to control us, and often does. But it can be overcome! When you confront your fear and realize you haven't died, you take ground. I once asked my friend, who loves spiders, to take a spider off the outside of their house and put it on my arm. I allowed it to crawl up me for about ten seconds. I didn't scream or panic, although my heart was racing. Once she took it off, I realized that they are not as scary as I had made it in my mind. Once I pushed past the fear, it started to diminish immediately. That was a good day!

DECISIONS

I believe that every decision we make is based out of one of two places in our minds. Either we make a decision calmly, rationally, and with peace (a place where you are securely loved) or you make your decisions based out of a place of fear. It cannot be both, no matter how hard you try.

Take a second and think about the last big decision you made. What place did you make that decision out of? Did you buy a home recently? When you decided to buy it, were you thinking "This home fits our family, it has enough space, and it feels right" (a place of love) or "The real estate agent said there were two other couples about to make an offer, so even though it's missing some things, and way out of our price range, I guess we should just jump on it" (a place of fear).

When I think about my time selling cars, I'm very aware of what place I made that decision from. We had wanted to do more things as a family and I was working part-time as a waitress when I got offered a job as a saleswoman. The sales pitch? "You'd be amazing at it and make tons of money!" That sold me hook, line, and sinker. All I saw was green, instead of really thinking about every aspect of the job. We had two young kids at the time, our youngest was two, and instead of considering all the time it would take away from the family—time with my husband and the kids, not to mention my friends—I just saw green. It would have been fine if I had gone to God about it and felt His peace, and if it was a career I felt passionately about, but I didn't go to God and didn't really look past each day.

I sold cars for a year and learned a lot of things. Some good definitely came out of it, but when I look at the big picture, it wasn't worth it. Why? My marriage was rocky for a bit, simply because I never hung out with my husband. My focus was not on him—and for that matter, it wasn't really on my kids either. I knew our daughter needed to be potty-trained, but I couldn't commit the time with my very busy schedule, and thought I would have to take time off just to do it. Turns out I left sales and felt an instant peace. That's when you know you've made the right decision.

The point is, that specific decision I made out of a place of fear and lack, of not having enough in my life, instead of remembering that God is a God of more than enough! He wants to take care of us and take all our fears and exchange them with His peace and everlasting love! Does this mean we will never have to work again? No. That is not what I'm getting at, but making decisions out of fear cannot serve you. When you make a "right" decision with the "wrong" mindset, it's all for not.

READY FOR CHANGE

Do you have a particular fear (or perhaps many) that plagues you right now? Are you sick of your fears taking the best years of your life? Have they kept you in the dark or in a little box for far too long? Well, today can be the day that you start standing up to your fears and take your freedom back. Maybe today is the day that you shake some of those heavy chains off your back and leave them on the ground, where they should be!

How can you do this? One good way to start is by asking yourself a series of questions before you make any big decision:

- Have I prayed about it?
- Why do I want to do this?
- Will this serve me and my family in the next five years? Or will it harm us?
- Do I have peace about it?
- If money was not an issue, would I make the same decision?
- Am I making this decision for me, or for another person?

This is a small start, but it helps to put things in perspective. Fear is part of human nature, but we do *not* have to let it run our lives. Keep reading and start gaining your life back!

LET'S PRAY

Heavenly Father, thank You for loving me. I am sick and tired of fear trying to rule my life. I believe that with Your help, I can overcome these fears. I want to involve You in my daily decisions, whether they're big or small. I want to be ruled by Your love and make decisions from a place of knowing that I am loved. I do not want to make decisions based on my fear. I know that when I do, the outcome for me will not be good. You know me intimately and want what's best for me. Help me trust You in that. Amen.

CHAPTER TWO

BACK TO INFANCY

And [Jesus] said: "Truly I tell you, unless you change and become like little children, you will never enter the kingdom of heaven."
—Matthew 18:3

I BELIEVE THESE WORDS THAT JESUS SPOKE ARE IMPORTANT FOR US TO take seriously and meditate upon. What did He mean when He said we should become like little children? What is it about children that we need to become like?

Have you ever watched a child before? Taken a full hour and just watched them play? Their lives are very simple and they have such faith. Hence the term "childlike faith."

I recently took some time to watch a life-filled one-year-old boy. He has a mom and dad who love him dearly and have provided all his needs. I watched him walk around a home—which, by the way, was not his—with confidence and wonder. He just walked where he wanted and looked at things with a blessed curiosity. *What's that? Who's sitting there? Ooh, that looks like fun to climb.* And up he went on the coffee table.

There is a beautiful age at which a child has not yet had a huge fall and they are literally fearless! This one-year-old was in that stage and it was inspiring to watch. He stood on top of a coffee table like he had just con-quered the world. Then, once he made eye contact with his dad, he leapt off the table only to be caught in the loving arms of his daddy. Maybe his dad's heart was racing a little faster than usual, but the child smiled, got down from his dad's arms, and did it all over again.

Watching this unfold, my own heart beating a little faster, I admired the boy's sense of knowing he was loved and cared for and could leap con-fidently off a high height because he would be caught on the way down.

We are that child, God's daughter or son, and are loved and cared for more than we could ever imagine. Yet somewhere along the way, we let fear take over. Not only are we afraid to leap, we're afraid of even climbing up the obstacle to make the leap.

Really, we have nothing to fear. That is what my life, and this book, is all about: finding out who I truly am so that when fear rears its ugly head, I can tell it where to go and push through into being the person I was created to be—loved and free! Here's the best part: you were created to be the same, yet in a unique and special way.

CONFIDENCE LIKE A CHILD

Do you have a toddler? Have you ever had one? Then you may be able to relate to this point about childlike confidence and persistence. As adults, we usually take no for an answer. Or maybe you'll try one more time, depending on your personality and fear level. Often, we're too afraid to ask for something because we think the answer will be no.

Children are very different, and we can learn something from them about confidence and persistence. If my kids want ice cream, they'll ask, "Mom, can we get some ice cream?" If I say no, they will probably ask me at least a few more times, and then stop. Sure as the sun is yellow, they will ask the next day, "Mom, can we have ice cream today?" Once again, if I say no, this will not dishearten them. They may even say, "Well, then when can we get some?" To which I will come up with a day, usually within the week, and if I've forgotten on that day, they surely have not and will remind me. They will not stop until there's ice cream, or at least a time appointed when they can get some.

Hebrews 4:16 says, *"Let us then approach God's throne of grace with confidence, so that we may receive mercy and find grace to help us in our time of need."* It doesn't say, "Come timidly to God's throne." No, it says that we should approach it with confidence or boldness—in other words, like a child. God is our Father and we can run to Him with confidence and ask Him anything. We are free to do that as believers!

The Bible also says, in Ephesians 3:12, *"[Jesus's] faithfulness to God has made it possible for us to have the courage we need and the ability to approach the Father confidently"* (The Voice). It is really important to note that not only can we approach the Father with confidence, but the reason we can is because of what Jesus did and not what we have done.

This may initially sound bad, but when you realize that what we have and are able to do has nothing to do with us, and everything to do with what Jesus did on the cross on our behalf, then it is freeing! Because He died, we can live—*truly* live.

One of my favorite verses from The Voice translation is John 10:10, which says, *"The thief approaches with malicious intent, looking to steal, slaughter, and destroy; I came to give life with joy and abundance."* The New International Version says, *"The thief comes only to steal and kill and destroy; I have come that they may have life, and have it to the full"* (emphasis added).

The enemy's greatest weapon against us is fear. Our greatest weapon to combat fear is knowing that we are loved and have nothing to fear.

In the New International Version of the Bible, the words "fear not" and "do not be afraid" appear just over 150 times. Therefore we can learn to live confidently like a child and be bold in the face of fear.

FAITH LIKE A CHILD

So what does it mean to have childlike faith? Childlike faith is to simply believe. No questions, no rationalizing or overthinking things. God says He loves me, so He must mean it. If a child is scared, or afraid, what does she do? She runs up to Mom and Dad and gives her parents a hug. What do Mom and Dad do in return? Hug their beloved child and tell her that she'll be all right. They whisper, "You're safe in Mommy's and Daddy's arms. Don't worry."

Childlike faith can serve an incredible purpose. There is something to be said about someone who is book smart and has lots of knowledge, so that we aren't just

> WHEN WE PUT ASIDE FAITH IN GOD AND IN HUMANITY BECAUSE OUR KNOWLEDGE TRUMPS OUR FAITH, KNOWLEDGE NO LONGER SERVES US.

fools walking around. But there comes a point when knowledge no longer serves us but hinders us.

When we put aside faith in God and in humanity because our knowledge trumps our faith, knowledge no longer serves us.

Most of us, even believers, walk around with a mentality that life is just the way it is and it won't really get any better. In all honesty, we could move mountains if we could rise above our victim attitudes and believe, as a child, that God really does have a hope and good future for us (Jeremiah 29:11).

Truly I tell you, if anyone says to this mountain, "Go, throw yourself into the sea," and does not doubt in their heart but believes that what they say will happen, it will be done for them.

—Mark 11:23

RECEIVE LIKE A CHILD

I read a book recently called *One Way Love* by Tullian Tchividjian. In it, he says,

> The very idea that a baby might do something to deserve our love—other than exist—is laughable. It's no coincidence that Jesus speaks so highly of children; He praises their ability to receive.[3]

To get rid of a fear, or to push through a fear that's keeping you from living the life God died to give you, you must be willing to receive love—His perfect and unconditional love. You may be thinking, "That's easy! Of course I want that!" But the truth is that many of us don't receive His love well because we don't feel we deserve it.

A child doesn't think further than "Of course I'm loved!" The end. There is no thought of, "Well, I pooped in my diaper and then smeared it all over the wall, so I guess that means my mom won't love me anymore." We

---

3 Tullian Tchividjian, *One Way Love* (Colorado Springs, CO: David C Cook, 2013), 160.

know that in a healthy child/parent relationship, this would be ridiculous. A loving parent would not withhold love because of something like that. Yet we too often believe this of our Heavenly Father: "Well, I've made a real mess of things. There's crap everywhere, so God must not think well of me right now. He must not love me very much." Even if we deny that we think this, deep down it's often what we believe.

This couldn't be further from the truth. Romans 8:38–39 says,

> *For I have every confidence that nothing—not death, life, heavenly messengers, dark spirits, the present, the future, spiritual powers, height, depth, nor any created thing—can come between us and the love of God revealed in the Anointed, Jesus our Lord.* (The Voice)

Take a second and reread that, because it is *good* news. Plus, loving us is who God is, not just what He does. God is love. Therefore, it is His very nature, His character, to love us. Not because of what we do or don't do, but because of who He is!

Children easily receive good things, and we could learn a lot from that. God has so many great things for us, including knowing more and more how much He loves us, if we'll be willing to receive His love like a child.

BEING CHILDLIKE

When Jesus was busy going from place to place teaching and healing people, some of the townsfolk brought their children to see Him. They wanted Him to lay His hands on their children. But the disciples started telling them to leave and not bother Jesus. Here was His response:

> **Jesus:** *Let the little children come to Me; do not get in their way. For the kingdom of heaven belongs to children like these.*
> —Matthew 19:14 (The Voice)

The old proverb says, "Children should be seen and not heard." Yet that's the opposite response from what Jesus gave. Anytime I get the chance to be with friends who have kids, I talk to their kids. I believe that children always have something to teach us, if we're willing to listen.

To be childlike and enter the kingdom of heaven, you need to actively pursue it. Would you like to have confidence and faith like a child and be able to freely receive like a child? I know I do. As with anything, let's bring it to God in prayer.

LET'S PRAY

Lord, thank You so much for Your amazing love. You say in Your word how important it is to become like the little children, and I want that for my life so I may experience all the goodness You have stored away for me.

I pray right now that You would help me to become child-like, but not childish. Help me to have every confidence in You and all You've done for me. I pray to have faith like a child in knowing that Your word is true and that if You said something, You meant it!

I also pray that I would be able to freely receive like a child today, especially Your great love. Thank You for working in my life and for never leaving or forsaking me. Amen!

CHAPTER THREE

WHAT DO WE TRULY FEAR?

When punishment is happening, it never seems pleasant, only painful.
—Hebrews 12:11 (The Voice)

SOME OF OUR FEARS FROM CHILDHOOD STAY WITH US, BUT FOR THE most part our fears change based on knowledge and what we focus on. During his first inaugural address, U.S. President Franklin D. Roosevelt said, "The only thing we have to fear is ... fear itself."[4]

Most of us have a few basic fears that come from a specific root. We'll go through them all but start with the first: the fear of punishment.

Now why do I say this one should come first? As grownups, we don't get spankings or timeouts anymore, but this doesn't mean the fear of punishment doesn't apply to us. Punishment comes in many different forms.

As a child, I was very afraid of punishment, mostly from my father, as he was swift with it and it usually left me with a sore rear end. My fear of being punished by him was greater than my curiosity, so I played it safe. It was more than just my moral compass kicking in. More than respecting my parents' wishes.

When I was young, we went over to my aunt and uncle's house one day. I was playing with my cousins when something happened. I'm not quite sure what the offense was, but I do remember that I had not participated. When my dad asked me if I had done said offense, I replied that I hadn't, and he thought I was lying. All I remember is that my dad got mad and me and yanked on my ear so hard that it felt like it had ripped off my head. From that moment on, I went out of my way to stay out of trouble.

---

4   History Matters, "Only Thing We Have to Fear Is Fear Itself." Date of access: March 24, 2017 (http://historymatters.gmu.edu/d/5057/)

I don't know how you were raised, but maybe you can relate. Perhaps you had it way worse than I ever did. In hindsight, my father probably had no other tools with which to parent me, or maybe he was having a bad day, but it still bears addressing.

How can we, as adults who have no one to really answer to, be afraid of punishment? Easy! We are afraid of disappointing people and the different methods they'll use to punish us for it. For example, if we don't talk to a friend for a long time, they may talk bad about us behind our back. If we don't measure up at work, we may not be promoted (or we'll even be demoted). If we aren't successful in the eyes of our parents, even one, they may not be proud of us. All these unique forms of punishment can be very real to us.

Consequences. That's it; we're afraid of negative consequences, which is another way of talking about the fear of punishment. This fear limits our freedom to make choices. Now there's a thought.

For the past two years, I've been on a journey to find out just how much God loves me. Would you believe it, I keep on learning new things, experiencing new waves of unconditional love and the freedom to live and choose. I still have a long way to go, but I'm excited about how far I've come and what treasures I have yet to discover.

This chapter—well, actually this whole book—is based on one specific verse:

> Love will never *invoke fear. Perfect love expels fear, particularly the fear of punishment. The one who fears punishment has not been completed through love.*
>
> —1 John 4:18 (The Voice, emphasis added)

Another version says,

> *There is* no *fear in love. But perfect love drives out all fear, because fear has to do with punishment. The one who fears is not made perfect in love.*
>
> —1 John 4:18 (emphasis added)

If there is no fear in love, then when we know how loved we are, the things we do won't be fear-based. Does that sound amazing? Does that sound too good to be true? It is amazing, and I want to share with you how this is possible so you can enter a new season of living out of love.

But first we must address what we believe now.

RELIGION

There is one type of fear I have not yet mentioned, one that keeps many, many people in bondage: the fear of being punished by God.

Your beliefs about God are vital to how you live your life. If you believe God to be a condemning deity who looks down on His pathetic, wimpy, and tainted creation, waiting to strike us down, then you most definitely will live either in full fear or rebellion. I've lived in both those places, neither good. In both of these places, you are shoving God away because you believe He is trying to shove you away.

Then there's the less harsh but equally damaging place of believing that God is a religion, meaning that He is more of an equation than Someone to have a real relationship with. You may believe that A + B = C. If you follow a particular set of rules, then God is happy with you and life is good. If you don't follow this set of rules, God is disappointed with you and life sucks. Here's the rub: not one person on this earth can follow all the rules all the time. If our salvation was based on what *we* did, no one in the world would stand a chance, because no one is perfect. The only person who effectively followed all the rules was Jesus Himself, yet He was still humble.

Religion bases everything out of doing. It focuses your worth as a human being on what you do. Since Adam and Eve sinned, it has been in our very fabric, in our DNA, to fall back into sin. Not that we can't be incredible in our human bodies, but we *will* revert to sin as we cannot be perfect by ourselves. Let me say that one more time: we cannot be perfect. If you are a perfectionist, that's hard to hear. But there is good news, so please keep reading.

Religion says that if we claim to love God, we will do what is "right." Religion says that every time we sin, guilt will tell us that we're wrong and need to repent immediately to be recognized by God. If religion was god, this god would say, "I see right now that you're dirty. Go wash yourself and then come see me. I cannot listen to you, hold you, and do anything good for you until you go get clean."

I believed this for a long time and stayed in this sad place of focusing only on what I did or did not do for God. Oh, and I believed that someone "holier" than me would always be doing more for God than I was, keeping me in shame and guilt and making me feel terrible, like there was no end in sight, no happiness to attain. I was in constant fear of not being good enough, not doing enough, going to hell and of being punished by God for past mistakes.

Religious pastors use fear to try and get us to do what is "right." If you don't do these particular things, you will not be blessed. Here's another way of saying that: "Child, if you don't do what I say, you will be punished."

This type of religion brings fear, shame, guilt, punishment, and death. Do those sound like good things to you? Well, here's something very interesting: many "believers" think and truly believe this is good, that guilt is good and shame has a place. They don't! Not in the kingdom of God.

DOES GUILT HAVE A PLACE?

How can I prove this? Anytime you've done something wrong—let's say you broke the window playing baseball—what's your first reaction? "Oh no, I'm going be in deep trouble. Mom or Dad is going to punish me." It's fear, right? Then, when you're actually in front of your parents, where are your head and shoulders as you tell them what happened? Your head is down, your eyes looking at the ground, and your shoulders stooped. This defeated position is caused by shame.

You may be thinking that of course the parent should be mad and maybe even yell at their child. Maybe you think this is a natural process: do something wrong, be punished.

But what if this scenario played out differently? What if the parent said, "Oh my goodness, is everyone okay? What happened?" And then, after the story is told, perhaps they say, "It sucks that the window is broken, but that has nothing to do with my love toward you, my child. Now go hit a homerun!" How would this child feel as compared to the child who got yelled at?

They would have a sense of freedom, not fear. This child would joyfully continue playing baseball.

Guilt will only keep you in fear of making a mistake again—any mistake—as compared to being loved and free to make mistakes and keep trying.

Do you believe we are free to make mistakes? I do! It's not a license to sin, but rather freedom to run full-tilt ahead, not slowly scampering ahead while looking side to side out of fear.

If we only focus on not being punished—by God, our parents, our bosses, or our friends—we live in constant stress. Have you ever felt that? Felt like you're hoping just to not screw up so you can continue being known as good and valuable? I lived this way for a long time, but it's no way to live.

I'm suggesting that you live your life in freedom, not shackled by worries about not being in God's will!

When Jesus died on the cross for all of our sins, while we were still sinners, He abolished the law of being punished by God once and for all.

It's not about wanting to sin and doing whatever you want. You're free to do so, but it won't bring you joy or peace. God doesn't want us to sin because it temporarily separates us from Him. But we can be assured that every time we sin, it cannot separate us from God's incredible love and grace. His love and acceptance is far greater than any sin we could commit! When you know this and have a relationship with the living God, when you know you're loved, even though you're free to choose your own path, the only path you'll want is the one that leads to Him. It's absolutely incredible.

THE DECEIVER

The thief approaches with malicious intent, looking to steal, slaughter, and destroy.

—John 10:10 (The Voice)

The only thing that the devil wants to do is drag us down and make us believe the worst about ourselves. An even better scenario for him is to make us believe that God does not love us, and in fact will punish us. What Jesus did was come down to break those chains of bondage and free us once and for all.

When we live in constant fear, the devil is happy. He is even happier when we believe that fear, judgment, condemnation, and shame come from God, because then we will never fully trust God and live free, but rather stay chained down.

Shame makes you believe that whatever you've done, small or big, decreases your inherent value as a human being. To carry shame is to live dejected, thinking that you're truly not worthy of love. Do these sound like good things? Absolutely not. Shame is a very strong chain that holds many of us down, but I am here to tell you that it doesn't have to anymore.

Shame will not give you wings; it holds you down right where you are when the act happened, and keeps you there so you can never progress. Shame and guilt are not of God and cannot produce lasting change, ever! They can only drag you down into the pit of despair, which is exactly what the enemy wants.

BEFORE THE CROSS

I don't know if you've ever read the Bible, but before the cross was a very different time for believers. If you believed in God, whenever you sinned, you needed to shed blood to get clean again in front of God. Usually the blood of a lamb or goat. Something had to be done and punishment needed to be dealt.

Another thing is that only people who barely sinned, priests and prophets, could directly talk to God or hear from Him. These people weren't perfect, but they were closer to perfect than those around them. Once again, the standard was all about a person's actions.

This was all before Jesus died on the cross, but many believers live as if the cross never happened. This way of living brought judgment on many people, many nations. If you are still part of that nation, there is hope right now to be free. Won't you join me in that freedom?

LET'S PRAY

Dear Lord, thank You that because of what Jesus did, having died on a cross for all my sins and punishment, I can live free from the fear of punishment from You. May I remember the freedom this gives me to live a life walked out with You by my side. That is good news and I praise Your holy name. Amen.

CHAPTER FOUR

WHERE'S OUR FOCUS?

Finally, brothers and sisters, whatever is true, whatever is noble, whatever is right, whatever is pure, whatever is lovely, whatever is admirable—if anything is excellent or praiseworthy—think about such things.

—Philippians 4:8

WE CANNOT FOCUS ON TWO THINGS AT THE SAME TIME.[5] THAT MEANS, our brain can only focus on one thing at a time. Even if we're switching our thinking from one thing to the next quickly, it's still one thing at a time.

Something else to note is that we can choose our thoughts. We are not victims to whatever may pass through our brain. People may believe that our thoughts are random and cannot be controlled, but this is a lie. Even though a random thought may pop into our heads, we do have the ability to let it linger, to meditate on it, or to kick it out. The easiest way to kick out an unwanted thought is to bring in a new thought. Sometimes this is easier said than done, but with training and willpower, it's fully possible. With God, all things are possible!

FEAR OR FAITH

Whenever we do something out of our comfort zone, fear initially pops up as a thought. But we have the choice to let it stay and take over, or allow our faith to be stronger. Now, let me be very clear: I am not saying that this is always an overnight occurrence or that it is easy—but it is worth it. Faith

---

5   Jon Hamilton, *NPR*, "Think You're Multitasking? Think Again." October 2, 2008 (http://www.npr.org/templates/story/story.php?storyId=95256794)

is absolutely a muscle we can work just like any other muscle in our body. Maybe right now your fear muscle is stronger than your faith muscle, but with constant use, it will get stronger and stronger.

We can either live in the fear zone or the faith zone. I don't know about you, but I would like to live my life the way God created me to be, and that is boldly, confidently, and courageously!

> *God gave us his Spirit. And the Spirit doesn't make us weak and fearful. Instead, the Spirit gives us power and love. He helps us control ourselves.*
>
> —2 Timothy 1:7 (NIrV)

When you became a believer, you automatically gained the Holy Spirit, which Jesus referred to as the best gift. We have the power through the Holy Spirit living in us to control our thoughts, especially the ones that make us weak and pitiful. God gave us His Spirit, which gives us true power, love, and self-control. Even if that's hard for you to believe, continue saying it until you believe it.

> GOD GAVE US HIS SPIRIT, WHICH GIVES US TRUE POWER, LOVE, AND SELF-CONTROL.

FAITH MUSCLE

When I was in my mid-twenties, I didn't think I was afraid of flying. That is, until our whole family went to Orlando, Florida for the first time. We got onto the plane and I felt good as it took off. We had just finished ascending when the air around us began to get really rough. We started bouncing in the air, and at one point we dropped suddenly; it felt like twenty feet. I don't know that I have ever been more afraid in my life!

My husband was sitting beside me and I was squeezing the blood out of his hand trying to calm down. When that didn't work, I tried to meditate and see myself already on a beach in Florida. My mind kept going to every little movement the plane made, while my kids slept peacefully beside me.

When I say I was afraid, I mean that my body was rigid, tense beyond belief, and I was sweating profusely. Have you ever had that kind of fear? It was debilitating. That three-hour flight, which made it to our destination just fine, felt like an eternity.

When we landed in Orlando, I was ecstatic that we were safe, but exhausted from letting fear rule my body, physically and emotionally. I didn't want to fly home again a week later, but I knew I had to be strong for my kids.

When the trip was over, I could have let fear take over and allow my mind to play all the worst-case scenarios over and over until I decided to never fly again. But I didn't want that to be my fate. I wanted to use my faith muscle and overcome this fear. Since then, I have flown many more times and have greatly reduced my fear.

Have all my flights since been perfect with no bumps? No. But I actively attacked my fear and told myself, *While on this plane, you can either be in fear or have faith, but you cannot do both.* So on my most recent flight, I chose faith. For the flight, I put my earphones in and listened to really positive, uplifting music and focused on the words.

When I got off the plane, one of the ladies sitting beside me even commented on how "joyful" I had looked during our flight, which proved to me that when we step out in faith—even (or especially) when it is hard—it most often encourages and uplifts people around us.

Be determined to build your faith muscle and believe that God is strong enough to help you through any of your fears.

No, in all these things we are more than conquerors through him who loved us.

—Romans 8:37

PETER THE BRAVE

The boat was in the water, some distance from land, buffeted and pushed around by waves and wind. Deep in the night, when He had concluded His prayers, Jesus walked out on the water to His disciples in their boat. The disciples saw a figure moving toward them and were terrified.

Disciple: *It's a ghost!*

Another Disciple: *A ghost? What will we do?*

Jesus: *Be still. It is I. You have nothing to fear.*

Peter: *Lord, if it is really You, then command me to meet You on the water.*

Jesus: *Indeed, come.*

Peter stepped out of the boat onto the water and began walking toward Jesus. But when he remembered how strong the wind was, his courage caught in his throat and he began to sink.

Peter: *Master, save me!*

Immediately Jesus reached for Peter and caught him.

Jesus: *O you of little faith. Why did you doubt and dance back and forth between following Me and heeding fear?*

Then Jesus and Peter climbed in the boat together, and the wind became still. And the disciples worshiped Him.

—Matthew 14:24–33 (The Voice)

This story highlights a few very important things about dealing with fear and faith. First of all, when the disciples were afraid, like all of us get in rocky circumstances, Jesus calmly said, *"Be still. It is I. You have nothing to fear."* Jesus said it back then, but it is just as true to us today, in our current circumstances, as it was back then.

When we are afraid, we need to take a moment to be still and realize who is on our side at the first sign of fear.

If God is for us, who can be against us?

—Romans 8:31

Also, Peter didn't believe it was Jesus, so he asked Him to prove it. Jesus replied, "Come."

When we step out in faith, it's important to know that it is Jesus calling us, that it is the will of God. When we know God is calling us to do something, He always equips us to do it. He told Peter to be bold in this situation, to defy gravity and the laws of physics and walk on water to Him. Jesus may not ask us to walk on water, but He will probably ask us to do something that's outside our comfort zone. But again, He will equip us to do it. We can be assured of that.

Then notice how Peter stepped out of the boat and walked on water. Why? Because not only did he know he was loved by the One who had asked him to do this impossible task, but his eyes were fixed and focused on Jesus! The second Peter took his focus off Jesus and thought about the ridiculousness of what he was doing, he allowed fear to take over. He focused on how strong the wind was and the waves beneath him, and as a result what happened? He started to sink.

We all experience rough patches in our lives, some rougher than others, but where is our focus? If it is simply on our circumstances and the environment—the wind and the waves—we will sink. It's inevitable. Or we can choose to focus on Jesus and end up doing something great, like even walking on water!

What happened to Peter when he started to sink? He cried out, just like we do when we feel the world crashing in on us. We often cry out to God. Notice Jesus's response. Did He let Peter fall in the water? Did He let Peter drown to teach him a lesson? No. Immediately Jesus reached out for Peter and caught him.

We will experience hard times in life, and fear will win sometimes, but it is so freeing to know that when we are weak, He is strong, and He will always catch us when we fall. He loves us and will help us through the dark, so long as we let Him.

Do you want to live a life where fear has no power and you are free to be courageous? Do you want to stand tall and tell fear where to go when it comes knocking? Overcoming fear requires a conscious effort, so if you will be so bold, let's ask God to help us.

LET'S PRAY

Loving Father, I want to do great things for You and I want to be bold and courageous! I pray right now that I will remember that You gave me Your Holy Spirit and therefore gave me a spirit of power, love, and self-discipline. You have given me the power to say no to fear and yes to faith! I believe this and thank You for giving me the best gift ever, Your Holy Spirit, to guide me in my everyday life.

When things get hard, I know that You will always catch me and I thank You for that. I declare today that I will choose faith over fear, Your way over mine. May I hear Your voice when You ask me to step out of the boat and give me the courage to do so! My confidence is in You and You alone. Amen!

CHAPTER FIVE

SPAWN OF FEAR

Therefore, now no condemnation awaits those who are living in Jesus the Anointed, the Liberating King, because when you live in the Anointed One, Jesus, a new law takes effect.

—Romans 8:1–2 (The Voice)

WE TALKED ABOUT HAVING YOUR FOCUS ON ONLY ONE THING AT A TIME, and the same goes for the next concept I'll be talking about. Fear has produced very effective offspring, and their names are guilt, shame, and condemnation. Let's go a bit deeper and explore their roots.

I know of many Christians who believe that guilt comes from God. I do not believe so, and let me share why. We'll refer to the main verse of the book first:

There is no fear in love. But perfect love drives out all fear, because fear has to do with punishment. The one who fears is not made perfect in love.

—1 John 4:18 (emphasis added)

GUILT

If guilt was an initial reminder of something we did wrong and then prompted an immediate action to right the wrong, it wouldn't be so bad.

Guilt is described as "a feeling of responsibility or remorse for some offense, crime, wrong, etc., whether real or imagined."[6] On this earth, if you

---

6 *Dictionary.com,* "Guilt." Date of access: October 30, 2016 (dictionary.com/browse/guilt).

are caught doing something against the law, you are guilty. What ensues after that is a punishment. But if you are doing something not against the law but against your own moral code of ethics or a religious doctrine, you merely *feel* guilty for it. Here's the thing: when you feel guilty for something you did but don't receive a punishment, like being thrown in jail, you often make up your own punishment, whether that's feeling bad all the time or something else. These are chains we put on ourselves, not that God puts on us. We are weighed down by guilt.

Guilt focuses not only on what we have done wrong in the present, but also in the past. The focus is on how bad we are and the punishment that must come next; therefore, all you can see is the wrong and not who you are in Christ. Christ took all of our punishment when He died on the cross so that we wouldn't have to pay with our souls. When guilt is the focus, there is no grace. And without grace, we are all doomed.

The book of Romans clearly outlines this concept of sin and guilt and the reconciling power of God's grace. Perfect love, also known as God, drives out all fear, especially any fear that has to do with punishment. Guilt is our sense of deserving punishment. We see the difference between guilt and grace in Romans.

When the law came into the picture, sin grew and grew; but wherever sin grew and spread, God's grace was there in fuller, greater measure. No matter how much sin crept in, there was always more grace.
—Romans 5:20 (The Voice)

You may be thinking that if we don't feel guilt, especially as a society as a whole, we have a license to run around and commit whatever sin we want, whether that's steal, murder, lie, cheat, etc. This freedom has the opposite effect, I assure you.

Just look at the story of Zacchaeus. Zacchaeus was a tax collector, a so-called bad man of the day who cheated people out of their money. When Jesus saw him, all He said was, *"[H]urry down from that tree because I need to stay at your house tonight"* (Luke 19:5, The Voice). No guilt, no judgment, no asking to right his wrongs first.

Zacchaeus's reaction to this love is *"Lord, I am giving half of my goods to the poor, and whomever I have cheated I will pay back four times what I took"* (Luke 19:8, The Voice).

I think Tullian Tchividjian said it best:

> Jesus didn't force, coerce, or guilt Zacchaeus into giving back what he stole; He just loved him. And yet the natural fruit of this one-way love turned out to be far more extravagant than anything Christ would have suggested.[7]

Zacchaeus gave naturally, because he felt the absolute love and acceptance of Jesus. It's amazing what grace will do. Instead of guilt freeing us, it binds us down, allowing us only to focus on the negative, while grace, the thing that would supposedly prompt terror and bad deeds, is what truly frees us.

> *Now sin and death no longer define us, but grace does: God's favor has been given freely to us through His Son, Jesus, who liberates us from sin's power.*
>
> —Romans 6:15 (The Voice)

One more thing. With guilt comes a sense that we deserve punishment, and that once we serve that punishment we will be made right. We then become our own savior. If we could save ourselves by doing such-and-such to be made right again or holy, we wouldn't need God. But we truly do need God, every day of our lives.

SHAME

We may initially think that guilt and shame are the same thing, but they are not. In an article written by clinical psychologist Dr. Joseph Burgo, who has been practicing psychotherapy for more than thirty years, he explains.

---

7   Tullian Tchividjian, *One Way Love* (Colorado Springs, CO: David C Cook, 2013), 127.

Shame reflects how we feel about ourselves and guilt involves an awareness that our actions have injured someone else. In other words, shame relates to self, guilt to others.[8]

Shame is defined as "the painful feeling arising from the consciousness of something dishonorable, improper."[9] Also, "to cover with disgrace."[10] Notice the words *painful feeling*. Shame can and does physically hurt. It is a terrible feeling that can only weigh us down, debilitate us, or cause us to do great harm.

Shame is usually established at an early age, but it doesn't always have to be. I once read a brilliant article that describes it perfectly. The author, Holly VanScot, quotes Dr. Marilyn J. Sorensen, a researcher who has been studying low self-esteem for nearly forty years. Sorensen says,

> "Early in life, individuals develop an internalized view of themselves as adequate or inadequate within the world," [Sorensen] said. "Children who are continually criticized, severely punished, neglected, abandoned, or in other ways abused or mistreated get the message that they do not 'fit' in the world—that they are inadequate, inferior or unworthy."
>
> These feelings of inferiority are the genesis of low self-esteem, Sorenson says.
>
> "Individuals with low self-esteem become overly sensitive and fearful in many situations," she said. "They are afraid they won't know the rules or that they've blundered, misspoken or acted in ways others might consider inappropriate. Or they might perceive that others reject or are critical of them."

---

8   Dr. Joseph Burgo, *Psychology Today*, "The Difference Between Guilt and Shame." May 30, 2013 (www.psychologytoday.com/blog/shame/201305/the-difference-between-guilt-and-shame).

9   *Dictionary.com*, "Shame." Date of access: February 26, 2017 (http://www.dictionary.com/browse/shame)

10 Ibid.

Once low self-esteem is formed, the person becomes hypersensitive—they experience "self-esteem attacks" that take the form of embarrassment or shame, Sorenson adds.

"Unlike guilt, which is the feeling of doing something wrong," she said, "shame is the feeling of being something wrong. When a person experiences shame, they feel 'there is something basically wrong with me.'"[11]

Shame goes to the core of a person. It is aimed right at the heart. Instead of acceptance, shame is rejection. Instead of love, shame causes extreme fear. Needless to say, I hope you realize that shame does not ever come from God.

When my husband Shaun and I discipline our children (yes, we *discipline* as opposed to *punish*), we try to let our children know that what they did was not acceptable. But they themselves are acceptable. What they did may have been bad, but they are not bad.

Another good point from VanScoy's article comes from another researcher, Dr. Aaron Kipnis:

Shame tends to direct individuals into destructive behaviors. When we focus on what we did wrong, we can correct it; but when we're convinced that we are wrong as a result of shame, our whole sense of self is eroded.[12]

I believe that shame is one of the best weapons the devil uses to keep us chained in slavery to sin and pain. He'll try to make you believe that God is ashamed of you. This is a bold-faced lie, but one we can get hung up on for years. If we allow it to, shame can ruin our lives.

Are you under any shame, even hidden? Ask God right now to free you from the bondage that it brings and start living free under God's gift of

---

11 Holly VanScot, *Psych Central*, "Shame: The Quintessential Emotion." Date of access: February 8, 2016 (http://psychcentral.com/lib/shame-the-quintessential-emotion/). Quoting Dr. Marilyn J. Sorensen.

12 Ibid. Quoting Dr. Aaron Kipnis.

grace. Jesus died for *you*. God created *you*. There is nothing wrong with you deep down. You were created with passion, pleasure, and a purpose. This is the truth! The shame garment you carry does not serve you, so why not get rid of it?

Shame is the idea of hiding something in fear that if anyone finds out, we will be ruined forever. Fear and pain thrive in the darkness. But the truth is that when a secret is uncovered, it instantly loses its grip on us. I know this because I have experienced it. Telling your secret to someone you trust, or even to God (although He knows everything about you anyway), is a freeing experience. The shame disappears. We have sinned and fallen short, but God's grace sets us free.

When we know we have done wrong, but that God's grace covers it, we turn our focus from inside to outside ourselves, to God and all His might. Then we realize how truly He is worthy of our praise, not out of need, but out of an elated sense of gratitude.

A few years into my marriage, I started to become attracted to a man I worked with. At first, I tried to deny it. Then, as I didn't tell my husband about it, I started to feel great shame. How could I do this? How could I feel this way as a wife to a wonderful husband who takes care of our children so well?

> SHAME ONLY GROWS INTO AN UGLY BEAST WHEN IT THRIVES AS A SECRET IN THE DARK. ONCE IT'S BROUGHT TO LIGHT, IT HAS NO MORE POWER.

I believed that if I told Shaun, it could ruin us. But by keeping my attraction to another man a secret, it only created further distance between my husband and myself.

So what happened? I'm not proud of this fact, but instead of telling Shaun the truth, he guessed it. When confronted, I could lie no more. I told him that it was true, that I was attracted to someone else.

Once this secret was out in the open, incredibly enough, it didn't ruin us. It didn't break us apart. Being free of the secret brought us closer together. Was it easy at first? No, we had to do a lot of talking and reconnecting, but it was *so* worth it. It made our marriage even stronger, and for that I am grateful.

Shame only grows into an ugly beast when it thrives as a secret in the dark. Once it's brought to light, it has no more power.

CONDEMNATION

Another tool the devil uses against us is condemnation, and there is a *big* difference between condemnation and conviction. Condemnation, coming from the root word condemn, means "to indicate strong disapproval of" or "to sentence to punishment" and "to declare incurable."[13] Basically, you feel so guilty that you are beyond repair. There is no life in condemnation. None whatsoever.

The root of this word, at its most foundational point, is damn, which means "to doom to eternal punishment or condemn to hell."[14] Take a moment and ask yourself, could this be of God? Does He make us feel condemned? If anyone had the authority to do so, it would be God, as He is holy and perfect, but He doesn't operate that way. Remember, God is love, and perfect love casts out all fear. So the fear of being doomed to hell (condemnation) most certainly does not come from God.

> *Therefore, there is now no condemnation for those who are in Christ Jesus...*
>
> —Romans 8:1

Once we have a relationship with the living and loving God, and only then, the Holy Spirit comes to "convict" us. Like I said before, convicting and condemning are two very different things. Convicting is showing the truth. From the dictionary, it means "a fixed or firm belief."[15] God is fixed

---

13 *Dictionary.com*, "Condemn." Date of access: Octeber 30, 2016 (http://www.dictionary.com/browse/condemn)

14 *Dictionary.com*, "Damn." Date of access: October 30, 2016 (http://www.dictionary.com/browse/damn)

15 *Dictionary.com*, "Conviction." Date of access: October 30, 2016 (http://www.dictionary.com/browse/conviction?)

and firm about blessing you, giving you constant hope, and empowering you to live with abundance.

The Holy Spirit may convict you of a sin that's hurting your life, or something that's harming you, but this conviction is never coupled with guilt, only goodness. God's unconditional approval is at the forefront of your identity. Then and only then will you hear the Spirit of truth, and that truth will set you free—unlike the condemnation that only wraps you in chains and binds you tightly. Do you see the difference?

Think about watching a child reaching his hand up to touch a hot stove. What would you do as a parent? Nothing? No! You would at the very least say, "Don't touch that! You'll burn yourself." You say this because you love your child and don't want to see him get hurt.

When we sin, we hurt ourselves. Take a look at the following example, when Jesus ran into a group of people. Once He showed up, He realized that there was a woman in the middle of a ring of Pharisees, and she was about to be stoned for committing adultery. This is what Jesus says to her:

> *Jesus straightened up and asked her, "Woman, where are they? Has no one condemned you?"*
>
> *"No one, sir," she said.*
>
> *"Then neither do I condemn you," Jesus declared. "Go now and leave your life of sin."*
>
> —John 8:10–11

See how Jesus loves on her, shows her mercy with no condemnation, and finishes with, "Go now and leave your life of sin"? He knows that being adulterous has harmed her, not only emotionally, but she almost died because of it. He does not want that life for her. God asks us to stop doing what is harming us, true, but it is covered in grace and love.

PERSPECTIVE

While the spawn of fear—guilt, shame, and condemnation—only keep you bound, the grace of God will truly set you free! The way we view life and relate to the world around us is based on the "glasses" we put on that day.

Are we wearing the glasses that only see the wrong in what we do? Or are we looking through the lens of grace? When we wear the guilt glasses, the focus is on us and what we have or haven't done. It's all on us and our behavior—and we already know that as far as human nature is concerned, our behavior will never be perfect. Therefore, we will continue to put on guilt and be pressed down.

But when we put on our grace glasses, we see the world not through behavioral patterns in us and others, but through what God has already done—on how good He is, not on how bad we are; on what He did on the cross to kill sin once and for all, not on what we haven't done. With guilt glasses, we try so hard to save ourselves through our own deeds, but through the lenses of love and grace we know that we could never save ourselves; we therefore turn to the One who has already saved us.

So the next time you feel anything close to guilt, shame, or condemnation, tell it to go straight back to where it came from and that it has no place in your life. Tell it that you are covered in the blood of the living Savior, Jesus Christ!

LET'S PRAY

Dear Heavenly Father, please remind me today that Your love is all-consuming and incredible. Please help me to remember that guilt, shame, and condemnation do not come from You. They only serve to make me feel less than what You say I am. Allow me to shake off the chains they bring, and instead be reminded that You may convict me of what is not working in my life. Thank You for the freedom that this revelation brings! Amen.

CHAPTER SIX

REAL LOVE

Most birds were created to fly. Being grounded for them is a limitation within their ability to fly, not the other way around. You were created to be loved. So for you to live as if you were unloved is a limitation, not the other way around.[16]

LET ME ASK YOU A QUESTION: WHAT DOES EVERY SINGLE PERSON ON this planet crave more than anything else? Money? Success? A soulmate?

While it's true many people crave these things, we all need to know we are loved and accepted.

THE CREATOR

Let's pretend for a moment that there was this amazing man… let's call him the Creator. As per his name, he created things, molded them. He did not create random objects, though; he put major thought into every single object he created. He thought about every aspect of every single being, creating them with passion and for a purpose. Every being had a distinct purpose for being created, carried great value, and was loved completely by the Creator.

This isn't just a nice story, but a reality. Our reality!

When God created mankind, he made them in the likeness of God.
He created them male and female and blessed them.

—Genesis 5:1–2

---

16 Wm. Paul Young, *The Shack* (Newbury Park, CA: Windblown Media, 2007), 97.

THE REASON

The reason I am writing this book is to talk about love. God's love. The love that changes hearts and lives daily. The love that rocked my world a few years ago after already being a believer for twenty years! The love that made me see everyone and everything, including myself, in a different light.

Have you ever been to church before? Heard any sermons on TV? Well, if you have, you know that there are thousands of topics you can talk about. There is baptism, faith, healing, wisdom, rebellion, etc. The list goes on and on. But I believe the most important thing for people around the globe to know and hear, on a daily basis, is God's love. It's the foundation on which we build all the other sermons.

It's all about love!

HOW CAN WE LOVE?

I think all of us believe, at least on a surface level, that Jesus loves us. But for a real heart change, we have to go beyond knowledge and be transformed at a heart level.

Attributes like victory over sin, having great faith, and healing come to us when we allow God to love us. Often we think that to be a good person, we have to love God. To do that, we first have to let God love us and let His love completely fill us. Then and only then can we love God and others.

We loved because he first loved us.

—1 John 4:19

HARD TO BELIEVE

I have another question for you: why is it so hard not to face shame, guilt, and condemnation day after day and instead let God's perfect and unconditional love change us?

Is His love really unconditional? The word unconditional means "with no terms." To expand on this meaning, note that the word unconditional means there are no constrictions. Something that is unconditional is not contingent or determined or influenced by anything else. It is very hard for our human minds to grasp this concept. Why? Well, we see conditions everywhere we look:

- at work.
- at school.
- while buying a home.
- In marriage.

Everywhere we look, we have to do something to get something in return. We must work to get a paycheck. We must work hard and study to get a good grade in school. We have to sign a contract saying that we understand everything about a house purchase before we buy it. We must sign a contract on the day we get married, with a witness, to make it legal.

The only realm where we get something for nothing is in the kingdom of God. To get His love, we don't have to *do* anything! In fact, there is nothing that we can do to earn His love.

> *But God, being rich in mercy, because of the great love with which he loved us, even when we were dead in our trespasses, made us alive together with Christ—by grace you have been saved—and raised us up with him and seated us with him in the heavenly places in Christ Jesus…*
>
> —Ephesians 2:4–6 (ESV)

We can do nothing to earn the love of God. In fact, just as the verse says, we were dead. Can a dead man do anything? Contribute anything? No. We were dead and He made us alive in Him. Not only alive, but united and called family. Ephesians 1:5 says that *"he predestined us for adoption to himself as sons through Jesus Christ"* (ESV). If he predestined us *"before the foundation of the world"* (Ephesians 1:4, ESV), then He decided there's nothing we can do to earn His amazing love! How incredible is that?

Romans paints a bright picture for us:

For I have every confidence that nothing—not death, life, heaven-
ly messengers, dark spirits, the present, the future, spiritual powers,
height, depth, nor any created thing—can come between us and the
love of God revealed in the Anointed, Jesus our Lord.

—Romans 8:38–39

So nothing can stop God from loving us? Nothing? Nothing. Period!
Not only can nothing separate us from the love of God, but He has restored
our honor and worth. That means that, yes, we are forgiven and free.

EVIDENCE

Hearing that God loves us is a good start, but we are human, after all, and
often want proof. How can we really know if He loves us? Well, thankfully
there is evidence left throughout the Bible.

I am going to share with you two stories of evidence of God's love that
really impacted me. The first comes from John 11. If you've ever read this
passage, you know that Jesus had a great relationship with the three siblings
Lazarus, Mary, and Martha. While Jesus was away from them, in a different
region, spreading the good news, He got word to come to their house as
Lazarus was very sick and going to die.

Jesus dearly loved Mary, Martha, and Lazarus. However, after re-
ceiving this news, He waited two more days where He was.

—John 11:5–6 (The Voice)

Jesus knew what had happened. Before He went to their home, Jesus
told His disciples,

Lazarus is dead, and I am grateful for your sakes that I was not there
when he died. Now you will see and believe. Gather yourselves, and
let's go to him.

—John 11:14–15 (The Voice)

Jesus also knew He would raise Lazarus from the dead.

Let's take a moment and think about this. Have you ever lost some-one you loved? Even as a believer, losing someone sucks! This was no ex-ception. Martha and Mary were close to Jesus and it still hurt them badly to lose their brother.

Four days after Lazarus had died and been buried in a tomb, Jesus went to Mary and Martha's house:

> *Mary approached Jesus, saw Him, and fell at His feet.*
> —John 11:32 (The Voice)

Mary was pretty ticked, and rightly so. She said, *"Lord, if only You had been here, my brother would still be alive"* (John 11:32, The Voice).

Can you feel her pain? Her grief? Have you ever felt this way before? Well, Jesus felt her pain and feels yours as well.

> *When Jesus saw Mary's profound grief and the moaning and weep-ing of her companions, He was deeply moved by their pain in His spirit and was intensely troubled.*
> —John 11:33 (The Voice)

John 11:35 says, *"As they walked, Jesus wept"* (The Voice). Really hear those two very powerful and impacting words: Jesus wept! This is the God of the heavens and the earth, who knew He was going to raise Lazarus from the dead, who loves us dearly and feels our pain and cares when we're hurting.

We know, as we read on, that Jesus does raise Lazarus from the dead. He knew He was going to do it because He told His disciples that before they even arrived. When Mary got mad, Jesus could have said, "Woman, you of little faith!" He could have said, "Why do you doubt my power? Come and see what I will do." Or even "Get over it!" But He didn't. Jesus looked into her eyes, felt her pain, and it pained His heart, so He wept.

He cares deeply for us in that way, too. He comes to you wherever you are, right now, and cares about it all, the big and the little things. If it matters to you, it matters to Him. You can bring it *all* to Him in prayer, with confidence that He is listening and wants to hear it.

ONE SHEEP

Another story in the Bible that has had a huge impact on my life is found in Luke 15:

> *Wouldn't every single one of you, if you have 100 sheep and lose one, leave the 99 in their grazing lands and go out searching for the lost sheep until you find it? When you find the lost sheep, wouldn't you hoist it up on your shoulders, feeling wonderful? And when you go home, wouldn't you call together your friends and neighbors? Wouldn't you say, "Come over and celebrate with me, because I've found my lost sheep"? This is how it is in heaven. They're happier over one sinner who changes his way of life than they are over 99 good and just people who don't need to change their ways of life.*
> —Luke 15:3–7 (The Voice)

Notice that this good shepherd doesn't think like the world does. The world would say, "Oh, it's just one sheep. I still have ninety-nine and I'm satisfied with that." This shepherd is not satisfied and truly cares about each and every individual sheep, so much so that when one walks away, He drops everything to go look for it. God cares so deeply about you that when you were lost, He went everywhere looking for you.

Imagine if someone in our world said, "All right, I'll go looking for that sheep." What would be the result once that sheep was found? Would they feel joy? In this world, we are reprimanded often or punished. People say, "Bad sheep, why did you run away? You don't get to eat for the next day so that you learn your lesson!" Doesn't that sound familiar?

We expect the exact same from God, yet what does He do when He finds the runaway sheep? He hoists it up on His shoulders! Then He calls all His friends and neighbors to celebrate, because His beloved sheep has been found.

Notice the difference? The world focuses on what we have done, as does religion, but our Good Shepherd focuses on the lost and rejoices when the lost is found. Our God is good and loves you so much that He would travel anywhere and everywhere to let you know it!

LET'S PRAY

Dear Lord, thank You for loving me so incredibly and unconditionally. It may be hard for my mind to grasp how wide, deep, and amazing Your love is, but I pray that each and every day You would show me more and more.

These stories were a good start to see evidence of how much You love Your creation, but I pray for a specific and unique wave of Your love today. Show me personally how much You love me, so that I can act out of that freedom. As I grow in Your love, I know that the impossible will be made possible. I pray for that to be my focus today! Amen.

CHAPTER SEVEN

THE LOVE MINDSET

Those who live according to the flesh have their minds set on what the flesh desires; but those who live in accordance with the Spirit have their minds set on what the Spirit desires. The mind governed by the flesh is death, but the mind governed by the Spirit is life and peace.

—Romans 8:5–6

LET'S RUN THROUGH A SCENARIO. LET'S SAY THERE'S A WOMAN—WE'LL give her the name Linda. She lives two days with the same agenda, but on one of those days she is insecure and therefore makes her decisions based out of fear. On the second day, she comes at life from a renewed mindset, knowing who she is and acting out of a place of being loved and accepted.

Linda is a wife to a busy working husband, and the mother of three children: Bobby, age 7; Samantha, age 5; and Lily, age 2. She is currently a stay-at-home mom. Her schedule looks something like this.

7:45 a.m.	Wake Bobby and Samantha to get them ready for school.
8:30 a.m.	Pile everybody in the car to drop the two kids off at school.
9:00 a.m.	Come home and start cleaning.
11:30 a.m.	Make lunch for Lily.
12:00 noon	Put Lily down for her afternoon nap.
2:00 p.m.	Walk Lily in the stroller with the dog on the leash.
3:30 p.m.	Pick up Bobby and Sammy from school.
5:00 p.m.	Make dinner.
6:00 p.m.	Eat with the family.

6:30 p.m.	Make sure the kids do their homework and have a bath.
8:00 p.m.	Bedtime for the kids.
8:30 p.m.	Tidy and relax.

DAY ONE: FEAR MINDSET

As Linda hears the alarm clock go off at 7:30, she thinks, *It can't be time already!* She hits the snooze button. Ten minutes later, she hears the annoying *beep, beep, beep* once again and hits the cancel button.

Better get up, she thinks. *But man am I tired.*

She walks to Bobby's room first, as he is the hardest to wake, and flips on the lights.

"Good morning!" All she hears in response are groans from under the sheets. "Please get up and get dressed or you'll be late for school."

All of a sudden, she hears screams coming from the girls' room, so she rushes up the stairs to find out what has happened. As she looks into the room, she sees that Lily has crawled out of the crib and is pulling all of Sam's clothes out of the drawers while Sam screams at her to stop. Frustrated, Linda picks up Lily and tells Sam to get dressed for school.

She walks to the kitchen to get the bowls and cereal going.

Our family is really outgrowing our house, she thinks. *This space is too small. One room is just not enough for both girls. Sam deserves her own room so Lily will stop pestering her.*

But her husband Robert just isn't making enough right now for them to even think about looking for a new place. Linda worries that if she brings it up, he'll just get mad and say that isn't in the cards. Plus the dentist had said that Bobby would need braces right away, and Robert's insurance wouldn't cover that.

Didn't he say his company was downsizing right now? she thinks. *Boy, I hope he isn't laid off. I don't know what we'd do. I'd probably have to get a job, making life that much more complicated.*

They would just have to make do.

First things first: don't be the worst mother of the year and yell at the kids again when they're being slow this morning.

The kids eat breakfast without too much mess, except for Lily. Once Linda feeds the dog and makes all the lunches, it's 8:30.

"Time to go," she prompts. "Everyone get your jackets and backpacks and get into the van!"

The kids get to school on time, barely, and Linda and Lily find themselves back at home around 9:00. As she places Lily in her highchair for a morning snack, Linda's mind returns to her thoughts and fears of the future.

Am I even a good mother? I seem to get so frustrated every morning and I often end up yelling at the kids. Bobby is in karate right now, but is that even the right venue for him? What if he wants to go into hockey? That will be a huge, time-consuming activity, not to mention the money involved. And what about Sam? She seems to like kindergarten a lot, but am I doing enough activities with her? Lily seems to take a lot of my energy these days, what with her being two years old. Speaking of her, I think I smell a poopy diaper. The neighbor down the street had her daughter potty-trained by the time she was Lily's age. Could I do that? Man, I must be a bad parent. Look at her, sitting in front of the TV while I do the dishes, but what could I even do better?

Linda grabs Lily out of the highchair to change her diaper.

Lunch comes and goes with food all over the highchair and floor. Linda then carries Lily off to her crib for a nap. She sings a sweet lullaby and quietly shuts the door.

Now that she has some time to herself, she doesn't know what to do.

Well, I should be cleaning our bedroom and start thinking about decorating the living room. But that just requires more money. The basement room also needs organizing, but I don't have the strength to do that right now. Maybe I'll pick a date to… oh wait, a month ago I said I would do it today.

She would just have to leave it for another day and hope no one noticed. If they did, she'd feel bad for letting down her family again.

She decides to take a bath instead.

As Linda sits soaking in the bath, she can barely let herself enjoy it; she feels guilty and has not relaxed at all. In fact, her thoughts are causing her even more stress than before.

2:00 p.m. comes faster than anticipated and she wakes Lily to go for their afternoon walk. She puts on a sweater, places a blanket in the stroller, and sets off with the dog in tow.

What have I done for myself lately? she thinks as the gentle spring breeze caresses her cheeks. *Myself? The kids take up all my time. I can't think like that. It's too selfish. But I'm so worn out!*

Her neighbor Hannah somehow manages to do it, though, and she has four kids. She's always smiling, too.

Her thoughts turn to Robert. *I love him so much, but I know that I haven't spent any one-on-one time with him in, like, six months. I wonder if we could afford a sitter so we could have a date night soon? Who am I kidding… Lily is at a really hard age. When's the last time I called my parents? By trying to be a good mom, I guess I'm becoming a bad daughter in the process. Ugh.*

They end up at the community park and the dog does his business. Linda takes Lily out to push her on the swings for a bit. Lily giggles uncontrollably, and for a brief moment Linda feels like a good mom.

At 3:30, the kids burst through the door with added energy.

"Mom, can we have a snack?" Sam asks. "We're hungry!"

"There's fruit in the bowl on the counter," Linda says.

Bobby chimes in. "But we want cookies or something else yummy!"

Linda looks around the kitchen. The last time she went to her friend Cathy's house for a playdate, she saw that Cathy had baked homemade cookies for her kids when they came home from school.

I should've done that, Linda thinks. *But who has the time? It's all just too much!*

"You can have what I said you can have. Something out of the bowl on the counter!" Linda realizes she almost yelled in annoyance. She feels intense guilt for getting mad at her kids and not being the right type of mother.

Supper is next, but she doesn't know what to make.

I could do lasagna, but I made that last week. We have all the stuff for it, though, so I guess that's what we'll have. Hopefully Robert and the kids won't complain too much. Or they can make their own dinner!

After dinner comes homework and bathtime, and they get through it without too much fighting.

As Linda reads stories to the kids, she has fun by making silly voices for the different characters. She prays for them and kisses them goodnight before going to the living room where Robert is already watching the hockey game.

I guess he'd rather watch this then spend time with me. I'll just finish clean-ing the kitchen. At least I made it through another day.

FEARFUL THOUGHTS

This may sound like a typical day for a lot of moms out there. I have lived days similar to that. I have compared myself to other moms, or other wives, thinking about what I'm not doing, trying to do everything right—and all on my own. Living that way can leave us drained and worn out very quickly.

But there is another way.

DAY TWO: LOVE MINDSET

The alarm clock goes off at 6:45 a.m., a whole hour earlier than Linda needs to wake up to rouse the kids. She heard at church last week that it's helpful to start your day off in prayer. That sounded like a pretty decent idea, so she has decided to give it a whirl.

She starts off by writing in her journal, thanking God for the first five things that come to mind. Then she reads a passage in the Bible and spends some time in prayer.

Lord, thank You for this day. Thank You for three healthy children and a loving husband who provides for us. I could attempt this day on my own strength, and probably end up feeling like a failure, or I could walk this day out with You. Lord, please show me Your love in a specific way today, and let me be aware of Your presence in all I do. I know that You never leave or forsake me, so when I'm feeling alone or overwhelmed, remind me of that. I thank You for loving me, and pray that Your love will fill my cup to overflowing so everyone around me feels it as well. Thank You that there is grace for today and that I don't need to worry about the future. As you said in Your word, "Because of the Lord's great love we are not consumed, for His compassions never fail. They are new every morning; great is Your faithfulness." I say to myself, "The Lord is my portion; therefore I will wait for Him." You are my portion, Lord. Thank You for that! Help me through today with Your mercy and grace and help me to be the best woman, mom, and wife I can be. Amen.

Linda feels a sense of peace wash over her as she takes her last sip of coffee.

She goes to wake Bobby and gently coaxes him until he's sitting up in bed, sure to not go back to sleep. That's when she hears the commotion in the girls' bedroom upstairs.

She takes a moment to pray, *Lord, give me patience,* then walks up the steps.

As she enters the room, she sees Lily pulling out all of Sam's things.

"Come here, baby," Linda says as she picks up Lily. "Listen, Sam, I'll clean this up once you're at school, okay?"

"Yeah, okay. But I really wish I had my own room already."

"I know, hun."

Placing Lily in her highchair, Linda begins to get breakfast ready.

The girls really could use their own room, she thinks. *I know that they're downsizing at Robert's company, though. Lord, thank You that I am able to be a stay-at-home mom right now. You know us well and I'm asking for a way to find a home with one more bedroom to fit our family better. I also know that Robert is a hard worker and we have nothing to fear because You know what's best for us. Right now I pray that Your will will be done and that Robert will get that promotion, or something even better. Bless his day as he goes off to work. Amen.*

"Who wants toast and jam?" she asks.

After breakfast, the four of them pile into the van and head off to school. Once Linda pulls up, she puts the vehicle in park.

"Before you guys go to school, I'd like to pray for you," she asks. "Anything special you want me to pray for?"

Bobby pipes up. "I've been dealing with Mark picking on me a lot and I have a math test."

"Sounds good to me." Linda turns to her daughter. "Sam?"

"Nothing special right now."

So Linda prays, "Lord, thank You for three amazing children and that I have the honor of raising them with their father. Bless them as they go off to school today. Bless Sammy in her class. May she have fun and learn lots. And Lord, I ask that you would give Bobby wisdom in how to deal with Mark and that they could come to a resolution today. I pray protection over him and ask that he remembers everything that we studied for his math test. Also, bless my time with Lily today. Amen!" She opens her eyes. "Love you guys. Have a great day!"

"Love you, Mom!" the kids reply.

Once Linda gets home and starts washing the dishes, she thinks through a list of all the people who may need prayer today. She speaks blessings under her breath.

Feeling loved and spontaneous, Linda lifts Lily out of her highchair and swings her around, dancing to her favorite song. After a while, out of breath yet feeling good, Linda smells Lily's dirty diaper.

The neighbor down the street had her daughter potty-trained by the time she was Lily's age, Linda thinks as she finishes changing the diaper. *But that's her and this is my life. Lord, let me keep my eyes and mind focused on You. I know that when I get into comparing mode, I end up feeling like a bad mom. You have equipped me to be these children's mom. Amen.*

With lunch finished, and apple sauce covering the floor of the highchair, Linda wipes Lily face. She carries Lily into her room and gently places her in the crib for nap time. After a sweet lullaby, she quietly leaves.

With some free time, Linda contemplates what to do next. *I should fold the rest of the laundry, and the basement storage room really needs cleaning out. Plus, the living room could use redecorating.*

Suddenly, she begins to feel overwhelmed.

Wait, too many thoughts at one time! Finishing one or all of those tasks will not give me value or worth. I need to check my motive. Yes, those things need to get done, but what can I manage right now? Well, a quick bubble bath sounds like a good start.

So that's exactly what she did. And as she soaked in that warm sudsy water, she felt her residual stress melt away.

After she got out, feeling great, she realized that she did have the capacity to clean that storage room. So she did, with no feelings of guilt.

Once Lily woke, Linda took her and the dog to the park. They played, ran around, and were silly for a good hour. As they walked back, Linda's friend Gracie popped into her head. Gracie had been going through a rough month, with her father passing away.

I think I'll bake her something tonight and bring it over.

When Bobby and Sam got home from school, they were hungry.

"Well, I was going to bake something for Aunt Gracie anyway," Linda said. "Would you like to help me with the cookies? You can eat a few after."

"Sure!" the kids yelled.

After dinner, during discussions about everyone's day, Linda asks who wants to come with her to deliver the cookies.

"I do!" Sam says.

"All right, but when we get home we have to do homework." Linda turns to her husband. "Robert, could you put Lily down tonight?"

They drive to Gracie's house and knock on the door. As Gracie opens it and sees her friend standing there with a plate of cookies, she starts to cry. Linda hands the cookies over for Sam to hold and hugs her dear friend.

"This is exactly what I needed today," Gracie says after a few tears. "Thank you! I had asked God to show me a sign if He really cared anymore, and I feel like this is His sign."

The two women chat for a bit while Sam chews on another cookie. Then they return home.

As Linda sits in bed that night, she prays again. *Thank You, Lord, for loving me completely and everything I have. I pray for Gracie and her situation and that You would wrap her in Your loving arms tonight so she'll know that she isn't alone. Thank You for another day! Amen.*

THE DIFFERENCE

These two days are very similar. Where your mind is at determines everything. Can we just switch from one mindset to the other? No, it's a journey, but that journey is so worthwhile.

> *Do not conform to the pattern of this world, but be transformed by the renewing of your mind. Then you will be able to test and approve what God's will is—his good, pleasing and perfect will.*
> —Romans 12:2

We can transform our thoughts, which in turn can transform our entire lives. We can then see the world and ourselves through love, not fear.

When we expect good things, and pray about them, our God listens. And the best part is that He cares about it all, even potty-training!

Cast all your anxiety on him because he cares for you.
—1 Peter 5:7

What's the real difference between these two days? The first one's focus is inward. How is life going for me? What is good? What is bad? What am I not doing enough of? I, I, I, me, me, me. Now, I understand that we need to take care of ourselves. It's very important. But worry and stress usually follow self-involved thoughts.

The second day, because Linda took care of herself first by spending time with God, she could focus outward. Because she was filled to overflowing, and brought all her cares and worries to the Lord, she could think of her friend in need. She was reminded of how she could impact her kids, husband, and friends, because all her needs were taken care of. Even if she didn't have all the answers, she knew and trusted the One who did.

Knowing we are loved by the Almighty God really does make a difference. As you may have noticed, in Linda's love mindset, she still felt the urge to compare herself to others, but she immediately brought it as a prayer to God, instead of just worrying and causing a lot of anxiety.

I have lived both these days many, many times, and I can tell you from experience that the second one is a lot more enjoyable. God wants the best for us, but we have to be willing to receive it and know that we are worth it. Otherwise, life will continue to throw us curve balls. We will panic instead of bringing our anxieties to God in rest.

Would you like to start having more enjoyable days? Let's pray about it! Oh, and just so you know, even if your day starts off hard and frustrating, you can change it at any point by talking with God and including Him.

LET'S PRAY

Lord, You know me better than I know myself and You still love me unconditionally. Thank You for that! I want more of Your love, because I know that when I'm loved, I can trust You more easily. I want to trust You with everything, the little and the big stuff.

You are good and Your will is perfect, so I pray for Your blessings in my life, and that I would have eyes to see them. Fill me with Your love so that it may overflow into every area of my life—my family, my work, my relationships, and so on.

Renew my mind to think of Your thoughts and not my own. I declare right now that fear has no place and that I will pray about things rather than worry about them. Thank You that I can come to You at any time. In Jesus's name, amen.

CHAPTER EIGHT

WONDERING WHO WE ARE

Man's main concern is not to gain pleasure or to avoid pain but rather to see a meaning in his life.[17]

—Victor Frankl

THE NEVER-ENDING QUESTIONS OF LIFE, AND THE START TO EVERY Psychology 101 class: who am I and why am I here on this earth?

Is this question important? Absolutely, and it has been since the beginning of time. It represents man's great quest in life!

Think about this for second. Stop reading, and think about who you are, who you believe yourself to be. Is there one quality that's bigger than the others? Is it only one attribute? Is it a good attribute or is it something bad you did, or something that happened to you once? Do you believe yourself to be a good person, except for that one little secret you carry around and want to take with you to the grave? Or do you believe you're a bad person with a terrible record, and that change, if possible, is far away? How do you define who you are?

Whether or not we know it, we all believe that our value is based on one specific quality or thing that we do. When we believe that we are only one thing, like only an architect or only a mother, we find ourselves in dangerous water.

Let me explain.

---

17 Viktor E. Frankl, *Man's Search for Meaning* (Boston, MA: Beacon Press, 1959), 186–187.

1. IDENTIFYING OURSELVES BY WHAT WE DO

The most common thing we believe about who we are, and that we allow to define ourselves, is what we do. What is your occupation right now? What do you do for a living? In fact, it's usually the first question you ask when you meet someone. Right? Even when you see someone you haven't seen in a long time, like a person you went to high school with, you'll ask them what they've been up to recently, and where they work.

Maybe you're a businessperson. Maybe you're a store clerk. Maybe you're a movie director. Maybe you're a singer, dancer, or painter. Maybe you're a politician. Maybe you're the CEO of a big company. Maybe you're a writer. Maybe you're a teacher or daycare worker. Maybe you work construction. Whatever it is you do, whether it's something you love or something that just pays the bills, it's easy to think that what you do for a living is who you are.

> WHATEVER IT IS YOU DO, WHETHER IT'S SOMETHING YOU LOVE OR SOMETHING THAT JUST PAYS THE BILLS, IT'S EASY TO THINK THAT WHAT YOU DO FOR A LIVING IS WHO YOU ARE.

Hindus have a firm belief that whoever a person is born as, that's who he or she will always be. So if you were born into poverty, you will always be poor and homeless, and there's nothing you can do to change that. The same is true on the flip side, that if you were born into royalty, you will stay that way.

Whether or not we consciously realize it, in North America we often believe the same thing: that we will remain in the same condition as when we were born.

Let's say you were born in a middle-class home, so you think the highest you can go is community college, if that. You may also believe that the best job you can get is at some store, selling clothes or food, and maybe one day you'll be a manager. Now, are these bad jobs? No. But it's bad to believe that you are limited or confined to do a job like this.

Maybe you're a professional basketball player and you love your job. You fully let it define who you are. Or you're a singer and your life's goal has always been to become a famous singer one day. These are good careers, but what happens when you lose your physical talents? What happens if you have a serious knee injury that stops you from ever playing basketball again? What if your singing career comes to a crashing halt because you get a severe case of laryngitis?

When we let our talents define us, we find ourselves on dangerous ground. Certain talents are not permanent. They diminish at some point. Look at Wayne Gretzky. He was one of the best hockey players ever to hit the ice, but even his great talent had a beginning and an end.

Maybe you're the CEO of a huge company, or you just got a huge raise at the firm. Perhaps you feel a great surge of confidence over this. Your pride is fully wrapped up in your career. You believe that as long as you have your career, you will be important. There are outside factors, unpredictable factors, that could take that job away at any moment. Let's say the economy fails or someone with more to offer takes over your position. What happens then? I believe we can feel worthless, like our lives have no meaning.

The following research proves my point:

The overall suicide rate generally rose in recessions like the Great Depression (1929–1933), the end of the New Deal (1937–1938), the Oil Crisis (1973–1975), and the Double-Dip Recession (1980–1982) and fell in expansions like the WWII period (1939–1945) and the longest expansion period (1991–2001) in which the economy experienced fast growth and low unemployment.

The largest increase in the overall suicide rate occurred in the Great Depression (1929–1933)—it surged from 18.0 in 1928 to 22.1 (all-time high) in 1932 (the last full year in the Great Depression)—a record increase of 22.8% in any four-year period in history. It fell to the lowest point in 2000.[18]

18 *Centers for Disease Control and Prevention*, "CDC Study Finds Suicide Rates Rise and Fall with Economy." April 14, 2011 (www.cdc.gov/media/releases/2011/p0414_suiciderates.html).

During the Great Depression, when people's identities were shaken, suicide rates hit an all-time high. People believed they *were* their jobs and the money they made; when their jobs and their money were no longer there, these people were lost, so much so that they believed there was no purpose in living anymore. They ended their lives over it.

This is very hard for North Americans to wrap their heads around—that you are not your job or career—but I believe it is so important to never label yourself by what you do.

In my past, I have had many different jobs. Eleven, to be exact. I've been a babysitter, paper delivery girl, strawberry picker, dishwasher, waitress at three different restaurants, cook, gas jockey, teacher of first aid and CPR, journalist, saleswoman, and a publishing consultant. And these are only the ones I've gotten paid for.

Now, I'll be honest and say that when I was a gas jockey, running to fill up people's cars when I was twenty-three years old, it was hard for me not to be a little embarrassed. On the flip side, it was also hard for me to not get a puffed-up chest about being a publishing consultant. But I distinctly remember having a talk with myself when I was a gas jockey, telling myself that I was not my job, that I could go to work with a smile on my face and try my best.

I am not any one of the things I've done for work, and you are not your job or career either. You are something more—but we'll get to that.

2. IDENTIFYING OURSELVES BY OUR PASTS

Another way we often define ourselves is by our past, whether it's who we were or what we have done. There is a third: defining ourselves by what another person has done to us in the past.

Maybe you come from money and stature and are terrified of not meeting the standards set before you by your ancestors. Maybe you were born a girl and your family was trying so hard for a boy, and now you let that define you; from the beginning, you've let your gender cause you to be a failure. Maybe you were given up for adoption right after you were born and have struggled with feelings of not being wanted. Maybe you were an unplanned pregnancy and struggle with why you are here.

Whatever the case, perhaps you've let your past define you, stopping you from experiencing all the blessings God has in store for you. And yes, God made you! He loves you incredibly with an everlasting love.

Let me share with you something I struggled with for a long time. I come from a family of four kids, myself being the youngest. In talking to my mom, she told me that each of us were conceived while she was on a different type of birth control. We were all a surprise. My three older brothers were born very close together, so she was a mother to three young boys by the time she was twenty-one.

I think my parents thought they were done with children, but to their surprise, four and a half years later, my mom found out she was pregnant once more, with me. Three months after I got married, my parents, who had been married just shy of thirty years, then got a divorce. This initially got me thinking that maybe I had been a mistake, that I had never been intended to be born. It was a very hard time for me.

But then I found this beautiful verse that changed it all:

For you created my inmost being; you knit me together in my mother's womb.

—Psalm 139:13

That means that even if I was unplanned and unexpected for my parents, I was *not* unplanned or unexpected in God's eyes. He made me and meant for me to be here. The same applies for you! Whatever your beginning was, it doesn't define you or put a damper on who you are now, or who you can become. You were made by God with passion and a purpose. Hold on to that promise!

Another inspiring story of overcoming one's past is Oprah Winfrey. Oprah was born in Mississippi to a teen girl and boy who worked as a coal miner. For her first six years, she lived with her grandma in rural poverty. She wore potato-sack dresses and most of her classmates made fun of her because of it. After moving back with her mom, she was sexually abused by family members from age nine to thirteen. She ran away and became pregnant at only age fourteen, but shortly after the birth of her son, he passed away. Then she was sent to live with her dad in Tennessee.

Take a moment to think of all the things Oprah went through by the age of fourteen: broken home, poverty, moving all the time, sexual molestation, teenage pregnancy, and death of a child. Even one of these things could lead to depression. She easily could have let these things overwhelm her. She could have also let herself be defined by them—but as we know, she didn't.

Oprah moved in with her dad and started doing really well in school. So much so that she got a scholarship to Tennessee State University. From there, she went from working in radio to being a TV news anchor. She was not only the youngest news anchor, but also first female African-American news anchor. She then went from co-hosting a talk show to hosting one on her own. At one point, she was the highest paid TV entertainer and ranked as the world's most influential woman.[19]

Oprah didn't let her past cripple or define her. And you don't have to either.

3. IDENTIFYING OURSELVES BY WHAT WE'VE DONE

Often, because we are human, we make mistakes. Many of them. We allow what we have done in the past to define who we are now. How do you get hired for a job? Usually it's because of your resume, a document stating all the things you've done in the past. So it's very easy for us to define our worth by what we have done. Even in prisons, people are put in different sections based on what crime they've committed. The maximum security prisoners go here, the minimum security prisoners go over there, and so on.

Have you ever done something you aren't proud of but allowed it to define you anyway? Maybe you stole something once and now you live your life trying to make up for that one mistake. Maybe you slept around with a lot of guys, and now you believe that's just who you are. Maybe you left your girlfriend when she was pregnant, and that decision still haunts you, even though it's been years.

---

19 *Wikipedia,* "Oprah Winfrey." January 3, 2017 (www.wikipedia.org/wiki/Oprah_ Winfrey).

Whatever it is, we have *all* made mistakes. None of us are perfect, not one.

There is no difference between Jew and Gentile, for all have sinned and fall short of the glory of God, and all are justified freely by his grace through the redemption that came by Christ Jesus.
—Romans 3:22–24

Like I said, we are all imperfect. Am I saying that what you did is okay and good? No, I'm not. But I believe that through belief in Christ and what He did on the cross, we can be *fully* forgiven and redeemed from our past mistakes. We can overcome the lie that our pasts define us and realize who we truly are.

… as far as the east is from the west, so far has he removed our transgressions from us.
—Psalm 103:12

As far as the east is from the west? That's never ending—and that's the point. He has taken our past mistakes and erased them. They're gone forever! Does that sound too good to be true? Thank God, it's not.

We know this: whatever we used to be with our old sinful ways has been nailed to His cross. So our entire record of sin has been canceled, and we no longer have to bow down to sin's power.
—Romans 6:6 (The Voice)

Something I carry very close to my heart comes from Joyce Meyer's book *Living Courageously.*

A mistake is an event, not a person. We may make mistakes, but we are not mistakes.[20]

---

20 Joyce Meyer, *Living Courageously* (New York, NY: FaithWords, 2014), 184.

Never let something you have done fully define you. You are more than your mistakes or past failures.

The Adulteress. There's a story from the Bible that means a lot to me in this specific area of letting our past define us:

> *Jesus went to the Mount of Olives. He awoke early in the morning to return to the temple. When He arrived, the people surrounded Him, so He sat down and began to teach them. While He was teaching, the scribes and Pharisees brought in a woman who was caught in the act of adultery; and they stood her before Jesus.*
>
> **Pharisees:** *Teacher, this woman was caught in the act of adultery. Moses says in the law that we are to kill such women by stoning. What do You say about it?*
>
> *This was all set up as a test for Jesus; His answers would give them grounds to accuse Him of crimes against Moses' law. Jesus bent over and wrote something in the dirt with His finger. They persisted in badgering Jesus, so He stood up straight.*
>
> **Jesus:** *Let the first stone be thrown by the one among you who has not sinned.*
>
> *Once again Jesus bent down to the ground and resumed writing with His finger. The Pharisees who heard Him stood still for a few moments and then began to leave slowly, one by one, beginning with the older men. Eventually only Jesus and the woman remained, and Jesus looked up.*
>
> **Jesus:** *Dear woman, where is everyone? Are we alone? Did no one step forward to condemn you?*
>
> **Woman Caught in Adultery:** *Lord, no one has condemned me.*
>
> **Jesus:** *Well, I do not condemn you either; all I ask is that you go and from now on avoid the sins that plague you.*
>
> —John 8:1–11 (The Voice)

This story carries such beauty. Have we not all been caught in the act of something we shouldn't have been doing? Jesus asked these teachers of the law, the most respected people of their time, to check themselves. He said that whoever has not sinned, whoever is fully perfect, should throw the first stone. As per the law, the sin of adultery was punishable by death, yet the only one who was perfect, Jesus, didn't even throw a stone. Instead He said, *"Well, I do not condemn you either!"* Such amazing words filled with grace! The same goes for us today, and for you specifically.

Notice He didn't make excuses for her sinful behavior or say that it was okay. But he said that, yes, she was fully forgiven. She had made mistakes, but this adulteress was not a mistake herself; she was highly loved by the Son of God.

You and I make mistakes, but we ourselves are not mistakes.

Overcoming Abuse. Many people out there haven't done anything in their past to haunt them, but what was done to them in the past *does* haunt them. Maybe this describes you today. Maybe you grew up in an abusive family. Whether it was verbal, physical, or sexual, you grew up in a home where abuse was common. Now you are left broken, in a place where these lies try to swallow you whole, telling you that somehow the abuse was your fault, that you "deserved" it.

Let me be clear: that statement is a lie. Adults are supposed to be trustworthy to children. They are supposed to be a safe place. But when moms, dads, uncles, older siblings, or even "friends" of the family break that trust, it breaks something deep in a person's spirit.

Fortunately, I do not have personal experience in this particular area. I have a few people in my life who have gone through this, though, so I am very aware of it. God has placed vulnerable people on my heart, particularly those caught in modern-day slavery, such as prostitution. How are these crimes related? Just take a look at the statistics.

- Every year more than 3.6 million referrals are made to child protection agencies involving more than 6.6 million children.
- The U.S. loses an average of four to seven children every day to child abuse and neglect.[21]

21 *Childhelp*, "Child Abuse Statistics & Facts." Date of access: December 6, 2016 (www.childhelp.org/child-abuse-statistics/).

Children don't often have a voice, and child abuse is a silent crime. Think about that for a second. 3.6 million only represent the cases that are *reported*. Yikes. Like I said, when our spirits are broken, we get misguided ideas of who we are and what we are worth. Often anger comes out and it turns into violence as we grow into teens, or we believe that because we were abused as children, a broken life is all we're worth now. Our bodies, and what we can do with them, become a means for us to gain acceptance.

Most prostitutes have been victimized at some point by sexual violence. Eighty-five percent have suffered childhood sexual abuse, often incest.[22]

If you have been sexually abused, or even emotionally abused, as a child, you can gain healing and get your life back. What if you could be free? Guess what? You can! Finding a reliable counseling service is a great place to start, but just as importantly, you can ask God right now to start the healing process in you. He made you unique and amazing and wants to show you just how much He loves you and that you are more than your past.

Because you are special to Me and I love you...
—Isaiah 43:4 (The Voice)

4. IDENTIFYING OURSELVES BY OUR BODIES

We are more than our physical bodies.

Since there is a physical, material body, there will also be a spiritual body.
—1 Corinthians 15:44 (The Voice)

We have physical bodies, but we also have a spirit and a soul. These parts of us will never die, although our bodies will.

---

22 Melissa Farley, *Rapeis.org*, "Prostitution Facts." Date of access: December 6, 2016 (http://www.rapeis.org/activism/prostitution/prostitutionfacts.html).

So often, especially as women, we measure our worth by something that's subjective and fleeting. It will not last. I'm talking about our physical beauty. Men deal with this as well, but since I am a woman, that's what I will be talking about.

We're so obsessed about how we look and the need for approval in the area of looking good, but it will all go away someday. We start this idea at a very young age. According to my research, in the United States alone, over two million children are entered into beauty pageants every year, from ages two to eighteen.[23]

I have a young daughter myself, so this really hits home. What is going to happen when we feed to our young girls, not yet women, the idea that that what they look like on the outside is the most important thing? What is going to happen to them when they get last place in this competition—or anything other than first, for that matter?

The statistics tell us:

- Anorexia is the third most common long-term illness among teenagers.
- Teens and young adults between the ages of twelve and twenty-six make up ninety-five percent of those who have eating disorders.[24]

Case in point: when society tells us that what we look like is the most important thing, and that we are probably too fat, young women take extreme measures. They literally starve themselves to try measuring up to this unrealistic expectation.

Even if they make it out of their teen years and twenties, the media tells them that even though they're getting older, it's not okay for their bodies to start showing that. So they turn to plastic surgery.

23 *Occupy Theory*, "Child Beauty Pageant Statistics." Date of Access: December 6, 2016 (http://occupytheory.org/child-beauty-pageant-statistics/).

24 *North Dakota State University*, "Eating Disorder Statistics." Date of access: December 6, 2016 (https://www.ndsu.edu/fileadmin/counseling/Eating_Disorder_Statistics.pdf).

Here are some more statistics from a 2011 study:

- Americans spent $10.4 billion on cosmetic procedures in 2011, up three percent from 2010.
- Ninety-one percent of all plastic surgeries are performed on women.
- About 230,000 cosmetic procedures were performed in teens ages thirteen to nineteen.[25]

This is absolutely ridiculous, but it makes sense seeing as we are trying to gain what every person on this planet needs—love and acceptance—from something that doesn't last. Our physical bodies have an expiration date, and that's okay. We are so much more than just our bodies.

Also, not being in the exact physical shape we think we should be puts us into depression.

- Women experience depression at twice the rate of men.[26]
- The rate of antidepressant use in the U.S. among teens and adults increased by almost four hundred percent between 2005 and 2008.[27]

I want to be very clear: depression is very serious illness and if you think you have it, I would encourage you to see your doctor. Getting help is important and good. But the fact that our worth and value as human beings is wrapped up in physical looks—and a specific type of look—is dangerous. If we are even a little bit outside the box of what "beauty" is defined as, and that's where we get our value, we will do anything to earn that value. And if we can't look like that ideal, we can go into depression over it.

---

25 *Live Science,* "9 Interesting Cosmetic Surgery Facts." April 16, 2012 (http://www.livescience.com/36260-chin-plastic-surgery.html).

26 *Mental Health America,* "Depression in Women." Date of access: December 6, 2016 (http://www.mentalhealthamerica.net/conditions/depression-women).

27 Peter Wehrwein, *Harvard Health Publications,* "Astounding Increase in Antidepressant Use by Americans." October 20, 2011 (http://www.health.harvard.edu/blog/astounding-increase-in-antidepressant-use-by-americans-201110203624).

God made us all to look different, not to conform to some cookie-cutter design. We are each amazing and incredible in our own ways, and our physical appearance is only a small portion of that.

> *I will offer You my grateful heart, for I am Your unique creation, filled with wonder and awe. You have approached even the smallest details with excellence; Your works are wonderful; I carry this knowledge deep within my soul.*
>
> —Psalm 139:14 (The Voice)

God has approached every detail of you with excellence. You are fearfully and wonderfully made just the way you are! If this is something you struggle with, I urge you to ask God to start writing the truth on your heart about your physical beauty.

It is also important to be aware of what we allow into our environment—our homes, friends, and the media we watch. That's why I'm very conscious of what I watch on TV, what I allow on my Facebook feed, even the books I read and the music I listen to. I want to be sure that it speaks truth and that I'm not just trying to gain acceptance through "looking hot." This is not to say that I don't enjoy fiction books or watch comedies. I do, as I think there is something valuable in them as well. I just want to be sure that what goes into my mind speaks value to me and others around me, and doesn't simply put a price tag on my worth. When I was a teen, I let it all get to me.

> *You are so concerned about external things—like someone who washes the outside of a cup and bowl but never cleans the inside, which is what counts!*
>
> —Luke 11:39 (The Voice)

I also think about my kids and what I say to them. What kind of truth am I instilling in them? Is it inspiration or could it be something that diminishes who they are?

I went through a lot of self-worth insecurities, even though I was told many times how "pretty" I was. I thought that was my only sense of value, so I craved compliments to fill my need. And when I didn't get them, I would feel terrible about myself and beat myself up. I do not wish this for my daughter, so I'm trying my best to be intentional about what I say to her and what I call her. She is absolutely beautiful, so I tell her that often, but I also want to let her know how smart and funny she is, and reinforce all her other amazing qualities so she can be a confidant young woman and not seek attention from the wrong people.

Physical Impairments. There's another aspect of believing that our worth lies only in our physical bodies, and that is measuring our value by what we are physically capable of doing. Now to be clear, I work out three times a week at the local gym and also play volleyball once a week, so physical activity is important to me. It is important to anyone's overall health.

The danger lies in allowing our whole worth to be wrapped up in what we can do physically. Take a look at football players. Is football an amazing sport? Yes. But what happens if you've spent your whole life gearing up for a football scholarship at a university somewhere and then you get badly injured and cannot play football ever again? If your identity is wrapped up in only one thing—especially something that doesn't last, like sports—you are in dangerous territory.

About six years ago, I wrote on my bucket list that I wanted to run a half-marathon. Then I got to thinking, why wait until I'm older to run it? Why not run it now while I'm healthy and young? So in the fall of 2010, I ran my first half-marathon. I didn't train, and the last quarter was really hard.

The next year, I wasn't going to make that mistake. Starting in April 2011, I set up a program to train for a half-marathon in June. I ran that one a lot faster than my first half-marathon. The next year, at the exact same time, I trained and ran my third half-marathon and realized that I was coming to really enjoy them. I trained for another half-marathon in the fall of 2012, but due to circumstances I ended up only doing the ten-kilometer run. (I came in third place out of two hundred women.) In the spring 2013, I had my training schedule all ready to start up again and my knee started hurting after only a few kilometers. To make a long story short, I had an MRI done and found out that I had osteoarthritis in my knees and couldn't run anymore.

I had come to kind of define myself as a runner, and when I got this news I was initially really sad. No more running! So I let myself be sad for a day, and then the next day I counted all my blessings. I could still work out, walk, play volleyball, ride a bike, swim, and so on. I am truly blessed. Even if I were to lose my legs, my worth wouldn't be in those legs. I am more than my physical capabilities, and so are you.

Terry Fox. If you're Canadian, you probably know who Terry Fox is. If you haven't heard of him, let me share his story.

Terry was a regular guy who loved sports, so much so that he was named athlete of the year when he was in Grade Twelve. In fact, he wanted to become a Phys Ed teacher.

Early into his first year of college, he found out he had cancer. He also found out that his leg would have to be amputated and he'd need to start chemotherapy right away.

If sports was your whole life and the doctor told you he would have to remove one of your legs, something you need to do sports in the first place, how would you feel? Terry was initially devastated, but he decided that this was bigger than him. He decided to be an overcomer.

Terry got a vision after his chemo, one that could and did inspire many to find a cure for cancer. He decided to run from coast to coast across Canada to raise money for cancer research. He wrote in one letter, asking for funding,

> I decided to meet this new challenge head on and not only overcome my disability, but conquer it in such a way that I could never look back and say that it disabled me.[28]

When Terry started his run, not only did he only have one real leg, but he was met on the first day by gale force winds, heavy rain, and snow. He persevered and continued on. His original goal was to raise one dollar per person in Canada, which at the time would have been $24 million. He didn't run the whole way, because of the disease, but he did end up running 143 days and 5,373 kilometers. On one leg!

---

28 The Terry Fox Foundation, "Terry's Letter Requesting Support." Date of access: December 6, 2016 (http://www.terryfox.org/TerryFox/Terrys_Letter.html)

Eight days after Terry was forced to stop, CTV held a nationwide tele-thon, and just over $24 million was raised for cancer research.

Terry was only twenty-two years old when he passed away. To this day, all across Canada, schools hold annual fundraisers and have Terry Fox Runs in support of cancer research.

This goes to show what you can do when you know you're loved and where your worth truly comes from.

5. IDENTIFYING OURSELVES BY OUR TITLES

In wondering who we are, it is very common to grab hold of a title you have and believe it to be, essentially, all that you are. This can be the title of wife, husband, mother, father, brother, sister, auntie, friend, etc.

Can these titles be great? Absolutely! But there is a real danger in put-ting all your worth into one of these, as titles can and will change. What happens when they change? It's similar to losing your career or job when you have put full stock in it, but perhaps it goes deeper.

I've heard women say, "All I want to be when I grow up is a mother." Please know my heart before you read on. I am a mother of two incredible children who are the apple of my eye, and I love them to pieces. They will always have a special and inimitable place in my heart. I also believe that being a parent is the hardest and best thing ever! It is a responsibility I do not take lightly.

That being said, I've seen many moms lose their identities in mother-hood. Whether they are a mom or wanting to become moms, they wrap all of who they are into being a mother, to the point that everything else gets neglected in their lives—their husbands, significant others, friends, jobs, health, hygiene, everything. They even believe that when they suffer, they are being better parents. They see nobility in parental suffering.

Now, while being a parent is incredible, losing yourself to it complete-ly is unhealthy.

If you are not a parent yet, but want to be so badly, what happens if you can't naturally conceive? If this is the only identity you want and your vision is set, you will drive yourself into some sort of state—perhaps de-pression—over it. I've seen it rip apart marriages.

Or let's say, worst case scenario, your child dies. I wouldn't wish this scenario on my worst enemy; it is such a hard weight to bear. But if your entire identity was in being a mother, then you would be lost.

In reality, you are more than just a parent. It is simply one incredible aspect of who you are.

Best case scenario, you give up everything you've done, loved, and wanted to raise these beautiful children, but then they go off to college and leave you. Empty nest syndrome. I have seen this happen often. You don't know right from left, as your children were your world. Their departure leaves you in a crisis of trying to identify who you are again.

This can also lead to you not knowing your spouse anymore. For the past decades, you've had no time to talk, hang out, date, or have sex. The relationship has been stagnant for years, so the moment your child takes off, you're left living with a stranger.

My parents got divorced after I moved out and got married. It had been years coming, but now they had no reason whatsoever to stay together. There was no more conversation between the two of them and no distractions of children.

This also goes for children born to someone who's famous or well known in the community. These children grow up in a world where they are known as so-and-so's child. Trying to live up to the family name can be very difficult.

These devastations can happen anytime you allow a title to become your whole identity. Titles have their place, but they shouldn't carry your entire worth with them.

6. IDENTIFYING OURSELVES BY OUR REPUTATIONS

Now we come to our last point. Growing up, and even into adulthood, I struggled with caring too much about what other people thought of me. I couldn't handle the thought of someone not liking me. Maybe you feel the same way right now. Maybe you can relate to this feeling. Here's the crushing truth: you cannot make everyone happy. You simply cannot. It's not possible, and here's the great thing: it's not necessary.

Often we are so wrapped up in our reputation, whether good or bad, that we fear change. If we are not forced to change, it's easy to feel trapped by the need to maintain our reputation.

I grew up going to a small town church. I attended Sunday school, then youth group, and even got baptized at age fourteen. That was a great time in my life, but I lived a very rule-oriented life to feel good about myself.

When I hit the age of seventeen, my best friend started drinking, smoking, and doing drugs. I didn't want to judge her, so I fully accepted her and everything she did. In no time, I was smoking and drinking behind everyone's back. I hid it from my parents, brothers, and church friends. I never did any hard drugs, although I hung out with drug dealers and all my friends ended up getting addicted to crystal meth.

A lifelong friend who went to church and youth with me found out one day. She ripped me a new one and said I was such a disappointment to her. She couldn't believe what I was doing. At the time, I felt my "good" reputation go out the window and I fully embraced my "bad" one. I liked maintaining that new reputation. Instead of finding out who I was, and what my passions were, I allowed what people thought of me to define me.

I found the man I would one day marry at a young age. Shaun was in a band and was twenty-two. I was seventeen. We spent a lot of our time together. By the age of nineteen, I was pregnant. This truly confirmed that my "good" reputation was gone. But I knew that this life was bigger than just me, that there was someone else to care for now. This made me grow up pretty quick, and also care less and less about my reputation. Although I cared less, I still thought it a good idea to get married quickly. Shaun did not.

I was incredibly hurt at the time, because I thought, *This must mean he doesn't love me.* I know beyond a shadow of a doubt that my husband loves me. Back then, he was making sure that his motives for marrying me were right. He didn't want to marry me because it might make us look better, or because my parents said it was the "right thing to do." No, he wanted to marry me when he was completely sure and wanted me to be his wife, first and foremost, and commit to me forever.

It was great once I got over my silly thoughts, because then, when our son was a year old, Shaun proposed to me at one of his concerts, on New Year's Eve! And I knew that he wanted to marry me for me.

Now, nine years later, with two beautiful children, I couldn't be happier. Is our life perfect? Absolutely not. Is our life amazing and filled to the brim with God's grace? You bet!

CONCLUSION

Over the span of my life, I have had trouble identifying myself. For a long time, especially as a teen, I identified myself by my beauty and my body. That's where all my self-worth came from. That, and from pleasing people. I always had to make sure everyone liked me.

Now, as an adult, I often identify myself in two ways: as a mother, and by what I do. I try very hard to have fun with my kids, to listen to them when they speak. In those moments when they're getting on my nerves and I yell at them, I feel terrible. I feel like a failure. I put my worth into being a great mother.

My second source of value, which I put too much stock in, is what I do or what I've done on a particular day. I constantly have a to-do list in my head. This list changes from second to second. There is no consistency with it, which raises my stress level when I think that I haven't done enough in a day. This includes what I do for a living. I have worked at certain establishments where my work was "menial." I didn't care about it in the long run, but I did it to help with the bills. My self-worth was not high on those days.

I can get carried away. If I'm working a job that I believe is "beneath me," I may not feel the greatest about myself. Just last year, around my thirtieth birthday, I worked as a waitress at the local pub and grill. I was also working part-time as a journalist for the local paper. So in my head, I thought that at least I was doing something that was in the realm of my passion. Now that I work for a publishing company, it's easy for that to go to my head. It's easy for me to place my value in being a publishing consultant. But this too can change, and is therefore dangerous. I will explain this is detail in the next chapter, but I want you to realize that identifying yourself with things of this earth is easy, and it's something we all struggle with.

Let's say you have gained a reputation for being the toughest guy around, so much so that you go to jail for almost beating someone to death. You get to prison, thinking, *I have to maintain this reputation, even though*

I'd rather get out of this life. You believe that if you don't maintain your image, you very likely could die there. On top of it all, your parents think that you're just a lowlife, and beyond saving. The prison guard calls you slime, and you start to believe it. You take on this identity because of what everyone says about you. You fully believe what others have called you, instead of going to the true source of your worth. But we'll get to that.

Maybe you were broken and abused as a child, so when you became a teen, you ran into the first arms that would hold you. To your surprise, those arms were of a boy who said he loved you, just to sleep with you. Your trust in people went out the window and you started sleeping around a lot, looking for someone, anyone, to love you. You came to think that maybe this physical contact was the same thing as love. Your peers and co-workers started calling you a slut and a whore—and you start believing them. Before you know it, that's all you truly believe yourself to be. You're left wondering if you really could ever be loved, if this is as good as it gets.

I'm here to let you know that your reputation does not define you. It will change like the wind. It's so important to establish who you really are so that when people say what they will, you don't let those names stick.

LET'S PRAY

Dear Lord, it's so easy to fall into the trap of holding onto a title or label so tightly that when something goes wrong, I feel useless. I don't want my worth and value to be fleeting, like a leaf in the wind. Please help me. Show me that what I do (or don't do), what I've done, my reputation, my body, my heritage, and my job do not give me true value or meaning. I know that it is so easy to fall into the trap of labeling myself by just one thing, but You created me for more. Thank You, Jesus! Remind me who I am today. Amen.

CHAPTER NINE

KNOWING WHO WE ARE

Define yourself radically as one beloved by God. This is the true self. Every other identity is illusion.[29]

—Brennan Manning

WHEN WE PICK A TITLE, ACCOMPLISHMENT, OR ATTRIBUTE TO DEFINE us, it doesn't hurt God, but it can hurt us! It makes us vulnerable, and our whole self-worth can change on a dime. The confidence we have in ourselves can change radically in a moment. Our confidence in God never changes. We are then free to be, or not to be. Our value, our core worth, is solidified in the One True God!

So now we know who we are not, or at least we're getting a really good idea. We are not what we do. Whether you have had a huge award given to you or you have a career that you are excited about, or even if you are a heroin addict, you are *not* what you do.

Whether it's how you were born (or what happened right after), the mistakes you've made, or even something someone else has done to you, you are not your past. If you have done something in your past that makes you feel like a failure or unforgivable, remember that it is *never* too late to start making new decisions and to forgive yourself.

Whether you love or loathe everything about your body—your shape, weight, stretch marks, or an injury or inability—you are more than your physical body. Whether you have won an Olympic gold medal or your bizarre diseases have made the front page of every medical magazine out there, you are more than your physical body.

---

29 Brennan Manning, *Abba's Child* (Colorado Springs, Colorado: NavPress, 2002), 64.

Whether you like your current title—husband, wife, parent, grand-parent, volunteer, teenager—or really don't like it but are letting it define you—single, unemployed, widow—you are *not* just one title. You are not just a mother. You are not just a grandfather. You are not just a teenager. You are so much more than just one thing.

However people have labeled you in the past, even if they're still call-ing you this, you are more than your reputation. You are more than the things that people call you or believe you to be.

WHO I AM

Here are a few things I believe that help make up who I am on this earth. I am a woman. I am a wife to an incredible husband who loves me and our children. He is also the front man in a band. So yeah, you could say that I am the wife to a rock star! I am a mom to two children who have blessed my life more than they will ever know. I am an athlete who loves to find out how far my body can go. I also play volleyball in a rec league. I am a daughter to parents who are divorced, although that fact doesn't describe them fully. I am also a daughter-in-law to my husband's caring parents. I am a friend to many who have been flowers in the garden of my life. I am a sister to three older, amazing, and unique men whom I'm privileged to call brothers. I am a sister-in-law to seven really special people whom I've come to call family and friends. I am an auntie to three nieces and six nephews. I am an adrenaline junkie who loves to hike, swim, and go skydiving. I come from a small town where we wave and smile to everyone we pass. I am a proud Canadian. Oh yeah, and I am absolutely imperfect!

These are a collection of truths that help make up who I am. But if any of these things change, it will be okay.

DOWN TO THE CORE

So far I haven't mentioned the very foundation of who I am. Who I am at the core of my being—the heart, if you will—is a daughter to the Most High God. The same goes for you!

Consider the kind of extravagant love the Father has lavished on us—He calls us children of God! It's true; we are His beloved children.

—1 John 3:1 (The Voice)

As a child of God, the best gift and privilege ever bestowed upon humankind, is something that can never, and will never, be taken away. This gift was paid for by blood and it is finished. Each and every person on this planet was made by a loving God who cares deeply for them.

WHO GOD SEES

It's nice to read those words on paper, that we are children of God, and think it's a fine idea without causing it to penetrate our hearts. I find that the best way to know something at a heart level is to first pray to receive it. And secondly, to experience it yourself.

That's why I'm going to provide you with a few stories and quotes that have made a big impact in my life regarding who I am in Christ.

I have an incredible CD that follows the stories of the Bible, with songs about each well-known tale. I've really enjoyed a few of the songs, but the one that impacts me most is called "When Love Sees You," sung by Mac Powell.

It is sung by Jesus's perspective and expresses how He views us. We are so quick to judge ourselves and see what we have done wrong—and what we are doing wrong—throughout the day, but this offers a fresh perspective on who we truly are.

The devil wins every time we think badly about ourselves, or about all the sins we've done, and hold guilt and shame like a cloak over ourselves. The truth is that when God looks at us, He sees His perfect, blameless, beautiful children whom He loves dearly. When God looks at you, He sees His beloved!

As the Father has loved me, so have I loved you.

—John 15:9

Meditate on this for a moment. God loves His perfect and holy Son, who has never made any mistakes—and that is how He loves us, too. Truly! How can this be? Well, God provides many amazing examples of this truth.

I believe fully what it says in 1 John 4:16, that God is love. This doesn't mean that God tries to love us regularly or that love is a byproduct of what we do; it means that God Himself *is* love, that He cannot do anything other than love us, as it is His very nature. He is the embodiment of love.

When the world thinks of the word "love," many different definitions come to mind, and they usually get mixed in with lust. This is *not* true love. So what is true love? Here are the best examples I have come across, from the Bible:

Love is patient; love is kind. Love isn't envious, doesn't boast, brag, or strut about. There's no arrogance in love; it's never rude, crude, or indecent—it's not self-absorbed. Love isn't easily upset. Love doesn't tally wrongs or celebrate injustice; but truth—yes, truth—is love's delight! Love puts up with anything and everything that comes along; it trusts, hopes, and endures no matter what.

—1 Corinthians 13:4–7 (The Voice, emphasis added)

You may have been hurt badly by what you believed to be real love. Most of us have. But this true, unconditional love is different. It is so very different. Perhaps you've felt the real deal in your life, and if you have, you are very aware of what it looks like. It is like nothing else out there. Real love leaves you speechless and knocks your socks off.

WAITING FOR SHAME

I'll share with you the first time I felt that real love from another human on this earth. You already know that I was quite young when I became pregnant, and also that I wasn't married yet. I grew up in a small, church-going community. I knew most people in my town and had been a member of three out of the seven churches.

When I found out from the doctor that I was pregnant, my first thoughts went like this: *What are my parents going to say? What are Shaun's parents going to say? What will the town think of me?*

Needless to say, I was pretty afraid. I'd sinned, having sex before I was married, and this was the end result. I was definitely waiting for guilt and shame to get thrown upon me. I find that the best time to feel God's love is when we're at our lowest and expect the punishment. Instead I found His amazing grace!

We decided to tell Shaun's parents on a Sunday morning. They were to be our guinea pigs, the first people we would tell. It was about 9:30 a.m. when we knocked on their door unexpectedly. Shaun's mom, Jan, answered the door in her robe. Shaun's dad, Gerry, was sleeping on the couch. He quickly got up to get dressed.

Shaun and I had planned on telling them the news together, but once we sat down with his mom, he just burst into tears and started telling her. Jan was surprised and also started crying as she heard this life-changing news. Then, and I will never forget this moment, Gerry came tiptoeing down the hall, finally dressed and having overheard us.

His next words changed my life. He gushed like an excited kid on Christmas morning, "I'm going to be a grandpa?"

So simple. So beautiful! The only thing he knew was that a child would come into this world, allowing him the great gift of becoming a grandpa. He didn't say "How dare you guys! What were you thinking... well obviously you weren't thinking!" Which is kind of what I had been expecting. No. Instead he was excited!

That was probably the closest I've felt to God's love on this earth. Here I was, blatant in my sin, and all God saw was the beautiful outcome. This is how God sees us!

SINGING OVER YOU

Maybe you have done something that you think is unforgivable. Or maybe you think that you are forgiven but that God is still constantly disappointed in you and your behavior. I know many a Christian with this mindset, and it is toxic.

Our God smiles when He thinks of you. God has made His creation and it gives Him joy. You give God joy! Not because of what you can give Him or do for Him, but simply by being you.

The Eternal your God is standing right here among you, and He is the champion who will rescue you.

He will joyfully celebrate over you; He will rest in His love for you; He will joyfully sing because of you like a new husband.

—Zephaniah 3:17 (The Voice)

God champions us, rescues us daily, and celebrates over us. I get a beautiful recurring vision of the Holy Spirit dancing over me, and it is a beautiful sight. Have you ever been a newlywed? So excited to start this life with someone you madly love? That is how God views you. Yes, you!

> YOU GIVE GOD JOY! NOT BECAUSE OF WHAT YOU CAN GIVE HIM OR DO FOR HIM, BUT SIMPLY BY BEING YOU.

Will you have bad days? Yes, as a believer you will have hard times, times that confuse you, and days that suck. But we have living hope on our side and a promise of the good that is to come.

God has sent me to give them a beautiful crown in exchange for ashes, to anoint them with gladness instead of sorrow, to wrap them in victory, joy, and praise instead of depression and sadness.

—Isaiah 61:3 (The Voice)

A MEETING OF HEARTS

A book that absolutely changed my life is *The Shack*, by William Paul Young. If you have never read this book, I highly recommend it. Without giving too much away, I'll premise the passage I'm going to share with you. There is a man named Mack who meets God in his brokenness and has an incredible, life-changing weekend. As Mack and God speak, they have a great exchange of hearts and words.

> "But why me? I mean, why Mackenzie Allen Phillips? Why do you love someone who is such a screwup? After all the things I've felt in my heart toward you and all the accusations I've made, why would you even bother to keep trying to get through to me?"
>
> "Because that is what love does," answered Papa. "Remember Mackenzie, I don't wonder what you will do or what choices you will make. I already know. Let's say, for example, I am trying to teach you how not to hide inside lies – hypothetically of course," he said with a wink. "And let's say that I know it will take you forty-seven situations and events before you will actually hear me – that is, before you will hear clearly enough to agree with me and change. So when you don't hear me the first time, I'm not frustrated or disappointed, I'm thrilled. Only forty-six more times to go! And that first time will be a building block to construct a bridge of healing that one day – that today – you will walk across."
>
> "Ok, now I'm feeling guilty," he admitted.
>
> "Let me know how that works out for you." Papa chuckled. "Seriously, Mackenzie, it's not about feeling guilty. Guilt'll never help you find freedom in Me. The best it can do is make you try harder to conform to some ethic on the outside. I'm about the inside."[30]

Can you feel that? This is a relationship of hearing each other instead of judging before knowing. This is a real relationship with a living and loving God. A relationship so intimate, that when you feel that security and great love surrounding you, you wake up and talk to Him. You go throughout your day always talking to Him, about everything. Nothing is too big or too small to bring to God. You bring the good and the bad because you're not afraid of being a disappointment or getting a bad reaction.

---

30 Wm. Paul Young, *The Shack* (Newbury Park, CA: Windblown Media, 2007), 186–187.

This type of relationship is the difference maker. I've had people say to me, "Oh, you're one of those religious people." I'm quick to say no, pointing out that I have a relationship with God. That can get people thinking, more than just trying to follow a set of rules in fear of eternal damnation, don't you think?

Either way, this is the freedom to be who we were created to be instead of getting stuck in the bondage of making a mistake and disappointing God. This is real life instead of death. This is love everlasting instead of fear that the love will disappear.

This is the place where I want to live my life, abiding in God's great love for me and for the world! As Jesus encourages us, *"Abide in My love"* (John 15:9, The Voice).

UNCHANGING

Does this all sound too good to be true? This is the basis of the entire gospel of Jesus Christ. When you start to grasp how incredible, jaw dropping, and fantastic God's love for you is, you truly can't help but *run* to Him. Why wouldn't you?

Praise comes as a natural byproduct as you realize that our God is truly worthy of all our praise! Jesus bled for you! He got whipped and beaten for you! He died the worst sort of death, reserved for the worst kind of sins, and He would do it again in a heartbeat because of how much He loves and cares for you.

All of this was the plan of the Father. He couldn't stand to be apart from you for one more second, so now there is no more barrier. The only reason for a gap between God and you… is you. That isn't meant to add guilt, but rather the freedom for you to run through the wide open door and be embraced by our amazing Heavenly Father, every second of every day.

Being a child of God will never, ever change. Like Jesus said, "It is finished!" Make this your identity at the heart of who you are. A son of God! A daughter of God! Because that is what you are and it is *so* good. We are not slaves to this world or to God. We are not only friends with God, but we are called His children!

OUR FAMILY

Everyone grows up in some sort of family, whether it's one with a mom and a dad who pour love into their children. Or maybe you were an only child or have tons of siblings. Maybe you grew up with just a mom, or just a dad, or a grandma as your mom. Maybe you are an orphan and have no biological parents but adopted ones. Maybe you grew up in the system and have been a foster child all your life, or even homeless with no family to call your own. Whatever the case, you have an idea of what family means to you.

I have come to believe that every family on earth has their own little quirks or idiosyncrasies. Not even one is normal. But whatever your normal is, let's create a new picture: we belong to the family of God, and that means He is our Father and everyone around us are our brothers and sisters. But this family is in a kingdom—the kingdom of God. A kingdom needs a king, and boy do we have one. Our King is our God, our Heavenly Father. He is the King of Kings! Think on that for a second. If He is not just a King, but the King of Kings, what does that make us?

If we are His children and He is the King, then that makes us royalty. Men, you are princes. Women, we are princesses. Truly! Do you remember as a child wanting to live in a castle, wear a gown, tiara, and be a princess? Well, I do. But the truth is that this is exactly what we are.

Here's the sad thing. Many of us are royalty, but we live outside the kingdom, homeless and feeling alone. We're looking at the castle, wishing we could live there, when the gate has been wide open this whole time. Not only that, we have an eternal inheritance in God. Inheritance is defined as "portion; birthright; heritage."[31] This means that all of God's promises have been yours from the moment you were born.

> *You no longer have to live as a slave because you are a child of God. And since you are His child, God guarantees an inheritance is waiting for you.*
>
> —Galatians 4:7 (The Voice)

---

31 *Dictionary.com*, "Inheritance." Date of access: January 7, 2017 (http://www.dictionary.com/browse/inheritance).

When we start to know who we are at the core of our being, it creates an incredible confidence and security. It allows us to walk out in the world with strength and a confidence that cannot be shaken, because it has nothing to do with us. It's best said in God's word:

> *Those people who are listening to Me, those people who hear what I say and live according to My teachings—you are like a wise man who built his house on a rock, on a firm foundation. When storms hit, rain pounded down and waters rose, levies broke and winds beat all the walls of that house. But the house did not fall because it was built upon rock.*
>
> —Matthew 7:24–25 (The Voice)

That is who we are—unshakable—when we know who we are in Christ!

WHY ARE WE GOD'S CHILDREN?

Why is this the basis for our identity? Why is it important that we are His children? Why are we not merely His servants? The book of James starts off with this: *"James, a servant of God and the Lord Jesus, the Anointed One…"* (James 1:1, The Voice)

Why aren't we merely friends of God? That sounds good!

> *And living a faithful life earned Abraham the title of "God's friend."*
>
> —James 2:23 (The Voice)

That sounds like a beautiful title. And it is. But a foundation should be something sturdy, something that never moves, never falters. And that is why we are *children* of God first.

A servant is someone indebted to a master. They can be punished for not meeting their master's standards. Now that I think about it, many Christians believe themselves to be merely servants of God. When the love of God envelops you to the core and you experience pure acceptance, you want to do things for Him. Not out of guilt or necessity, but out of joy. Then we are gladly servants of God, willingly.

"Friend of God," while an incredible title, can also leave us lacking in a few ways. We are blessed enough to call God our friend, but friends, as we know them on earth, can change. You can stop being friends with someone. There is no permanent tie. God is a friend, someone we can confide in about anything, but He's also more than that. He's our Father and we are His children.

So again, why are we God's children? What is so special about that? Think of your children for a moment, if you have any. Can they survive on their own when they're born? Absolutely not. They need you, especially in the beginning. Children need their parents, or at least a guardian. Thank the Lord that He is so much more than just a guardian who's there to take care of our essentials. No, He cares about every detail.

You, beloved, are worth so much more than a whole flock of sparrows. God knows everything about you, even the number of hairs on your head. So do not fear.
—Matthew 10:31 (The Voice)

Just as children need their parents every single day, we need our God. We are lost without Him, yet everything is fine, even amidst the storm, when we have God with us. He is here to help. He is our refuge and strength. We don't ever have to do anything alone. The hard stuff, the easy stuff, He's part of it all if we will just invite Him in as our loving Father.

Children are bonded to us by blood, and we are bound to God because of His blood and what Jesus did for us on the cross. You can quit being friends with someone and you can fire a servant, but you will never stop being related to your family. Your mom is your mom and you are her child. The same goes for God. We are not casual chums, there to converse with each other here and there. On top of being God of the Universe, He is our loving parent who loves us so incredibly and longs to hear our hearts every step of the way. He knows us intimately. He also wants us to know Him intimately.

It all starts and ends with a willing heart, with just saying, "Yes! God, I want to know you more intimately!" He will show you.

Take a moment right now and ask yourself how you see God. Who is God to you right now? Is He anything other than a good Daddy? Are you afraid of Him? Do you think He's going to punish you if you don't do a certain amount of things for Him? If you think that you may be believing lies about God, ask Him to show you who He truly is, today!

SECURE IN HIM

Tullian Tchividjian said it best in His book, *One Way Love*:

> Who you really are had nothing to do with you – how much you can accomplish, who you can become, your behavior (good or bad), your strengths, your weaknesses, your sordid past, your family background, your education, your looks and so on. Your identity is firmly anchored in Christ's accomplishments, not yours; His strengths, not yours; His performance, not yours; His victory, not yours. Your identity is steadfastly established in His substitution, not your sin.[32]

Would you like to live in this security with Jesus as Your Savior and God the Father as your King? It is possible, and you can take that step into this beautiful journey right now!

LET'S PRAY

Dear Lord, thank You for loving me so extravagantly that You call me Your child. Help me believe that a little more right now. May I know who You are and the love You have for me.

The word says that I am Your child and that I have an inheritance. Lord, I know that there is nothing I have done or ever

---

32 Tullian Tchividjian, *One Way Love* (Colorado Springs, CO: David C Cook, 2013), 225.

will do to deserve this, but it is because of Your incredible mercy and grace. I thank You for this free gift and ask You to help me receive it more and more each day. Help me write on my heart my true identity, which will never change: I am Your beloved child! Amen.

CHAPTER TEN

GOOD FATHER

He destined us to be adopted as His children through the covenant Jesus the Anointed inaugurated in His sacrificial life. This was His pleasure and His will for us.

—Ephesians 1:5 (The Voice)

THE BIBLE DESCRIBES GOD MOSTLY IN MALE FORM: GOD THE FATHER, God the Son. In reality, however, God is neither male nor female. Now, we will not spend too much time on this topic, as I don't want to lose you here, but we are all created in His image, which is male *and* female.

So God created mankind in his own image, in the image of God he created them; male and female he created them.

—Genesis 1:27

Both genders, together, make up God. It's just a truth. So in this chapter, we will be aware of God as the Father of all.

If we relate God to our earthly fathers, many of us will believe lies. As good or bad as our earthly fathers are (or were), it pales in comparison to who God is.

BELIEVED LIES

When I was newly married, and twenty-one years old, my parents, who had been married for almost thirty years, separated, and a year later got divorced. Even though I was an adult, it still affected me. Before this point, my parents had lived many lies in their marriage and probably had had a lack of love for many years beforehand.

Why am I talking about my parents' divorce? Well, I believe many of you can relate. Many of you have walked this road, whether you were a child at the time or an adult.

When my dad divorced my mom, I felt like he and I were cut off as well. He still lived in the same town, so he was physically close, but I felt a void, as though he hadn't just left my mother. For me to relate God the Father to this feeling, I kind of felt like He would one day leave me and potentially disappoint me.

I had always related to Jesus quite well. I felt like He was for me and that He was a friend I could trust. But when it came to God the Father, I just put Him on a high shelf in my heart and closed the door between us. I believed He was untrustworthy, maybe sitting on a high throne, ready to judge me. So even though I believed in God, I decided not to think about that part of Him in depth.

Well, God is great at getting to the heart of the matter. He will not leave us alone, thankfully. One night, while the kids were sleeping and Shaun was gone for the evening, I just sat in my living room chair and talked with God the Father. I told Him that I was sure I had believed lies about who He was in my heart, and I wanted Him to rewrite the truth on my heart.

Within a few minutes, I heard God speak directly to me: "Sylvia, I will never divorce you."

In the dictionary, the word divorce means "total separation."[33] In my heart, I was afraid that God would one day, for whatever reason, decide I wasn't good enough and then make a break for it—that He would leave me to fend for myself. Hearing this from God the Father felt so amazing and beautiful, like a chain came off. My heart started to heal instantly.

I know that I'm not married to God and that He is not my husband, so I know how weird it may sound. Yet God's unique and specific voice was saying to me that He would never leave me or forsake me, that I could

---

33 *Dictionary.com*, "Divorce." Date of access: January 7, 2017 (dictionary.com/ browse/ divorce).

honestly trust Him to hold me and never let me go, like I felt that my earthly father had done to me.

I promise you, God wants to tell you in a specific and personal way that He loves you—if you will let Him. Allow Him to rewrite the truth upon your heart. You'll never regret it. He can do it, no matter how broken or shattered your heart may be.

I recently saw this fabulous cartoon:

Maybe your heart isn't just cracked, but shattered into a million pieces by the betrayal of another human being. But this I promise you: when you give your broken, bruised, and beaten heart to God, He can heal it.

SAVING OURSELVES

Let's take this a little further. Do you have children of your own? Biological, adopted, doesn't matter. If you are a parent, a loving parent, then you know (or can feel) what God meant by the term "unconditional love." When you have your first baby, you say to yourself, "How can I love somebody that I just met so much? How can I love someone this much? How can I want to do everything in the world to protect them even though they have done nothing for me?"

Ever felt that? I know I have. Sure, there are hard days as a parent, but this feeling of slightly understanding God's love remains.

As our child grows older, we ask them to start helping out around the house. When they are about two, we ask them to pick up their toys. When they are five, we ask them to clean up their room and make their bed. When they are eight, we ask them to vacuum and clean out the dishwasher. At twelve, we may ask them to mow the lawn and rake the leaves in the fall. You get the idea. As they grow, we ask more of them because they can handle it. These tasks will help them out as adults to know how to do things and survive on their own. We need to give them life skills.

As loving parents, would we ask them to pay the rent at age five? How about the electricity and phone bills? What about keeping the whole house clean all the time and never spilling or making a mess, and always being responsible for everything? No. As loving parents, we wouldn't ask our young children to be the parent in the relationship. We are aware that they are children and we are responsible adults.

This example parallels God the Father. Is He a loving Daddy? Yes, He absolutely is. So as we grow in our relationship, God may ask us to do things, but He will never ask us to do something we are incapable of doing. If God asks us to do something, He will give us the ability to do it, every time. He would never set us up for failure.

Also, just like a loving parent wouldn't ask their children to be responsible for everything, to pay

> WHEN WE ASK GOD TO HELP US LIVE EACH DAY WITH HIS GRACE, THEN WHATEVER IS DONE IN LOVE THROUGHOUT THE DAY IS A BLESSING TO GOD'S HEART.

for everything and clean the whole house, God will never—and has never—asked us to save ourselves. He sent His Son to live on the earth and then die for our salvation. He is not in need of us doing good deeds to save ourselves. This is what religion preaches, even if they are not always aware that they're doing it. In fact, God is much more concerned with our hearts than our deeds.

If your child, innocent and full of wonder, picks up a rock and hands it to you, what would you do? You would accept it. Does this rock benefit you? No, but pay attention to the heart behind the gift. After all, this rock is the one thing they have found and liked, the only thing they have—and they have given it to you! Therefore it's special.

When we ask God to help us live each day with His grace, then whatever is done in love throughout the day is a blessing to God's heart. It does not earn our salvation, but comes from a pure and loved heart, which makes it special.

GOOD GIFTS

If you, as a loving parent, would never ask your child to do everything to keep your household going, God would certainly not ask us to save ourselves. Shaun and I love our children, even when our daughter continues to bug her older brother and he continues to make a mess and not clean it up. Their behavior is not contingent on our love for them. I have tried to make that very clear to my children. Mom and Dad may get mad or frustrated when they hurt each other or don't listen, but our love for them never changes. We may be mad, but we love them.

This Bible verse perfectly outlines what I'm trying to say:

> *Which of you fathers, if your son asks for a fish, will give him a snake instead? Or if he asks for an egg, will give him a scorpion? If you then, though you are evil, know how to give good gifts to your children, how much more will your Father in heaven give the Holy Spirit to those who ask him!*
>
> —Luke 11:11–13 (The Voice)

THE RECKLESS SON

Most of you reading this probably know the story in the Bible about the prodigal son, but while reading it the other day, I saw it from a different angle. Let's read it together first.

> Once there was this man who had two sons. One day the younger son came to his father and said, "Father, eventually I'm going to inherit my share of your estate. Rather than waiting until you die, I want you to give me my share now." And so the father liquidated assets and divided them. A few days passed and this younger son gathered all his wealth and set off on a journey to a distant land. Once there he wasted everything he owned on wild living. He was broke, a terrible famine struck that land, and he felt desperately hungry and in need. He got a job with one of the locals, who sent him into the fields to feed the pigs. The young man felt so miserably hungry that he wished he could eat the slop the pigs were eating. Nobody gave him anything.
>
> So he had this moment of self-reflection: "What am I doing here? Back home, my father's hired servants have plenty of food. Why am I here starving to death? I'll get up and return to my father, and I'll say, 'Father, I have done wrong—wrong against God and against you. I have forfeited any right to be treated like your son, but I'm wondering if you'd treat me as one of your hired servants?'" So he got up and returned to his father. The father looked off in the distance and saw the young man returning. He felt compassion for his son and ran out to him, enfolded him in an embrace, and kissed him.
>
> The son said, "Father, I have done a terrible wrong in God's sight and in your sight too. I have forfeited any right to be treated as your son."
>
> But the father turned to his servants and said, "Quick! Bring the best robe we have and put it on him. Put a ring on his finger and shoes on his feet. Go get the fattest calf and butcher it. Let's have a

*feast and celebrate because my son was dead and is alive again. He
was lost and has been found." So they had this huge party.*

—Luke 15:11–24 (The Voice)

There's more to the story, but I want to focus on the first part. It sounds
to me like these two sons, who grew up in the same home, had a pretty
good upbringing, even a great inheritance to look forward to. The prodigal
son suddenly rebelled. He asked for his full inheritance. Now, to be clear,
people usually gain their inheritance only when the person bestowing it
dies. In this sense, the prodigal son was basically saying to his father, "You
are dead to me." He wanted nothing more to do with his father or family,
just the money and wealth.

What a terrible and selfish thing to do, no? But haven't we all been in
those shoes in one form or another, acting out of selfishness and greed? I've
done some terrible things without thinking of the person I would greatly
hurt at the end of it.

What's evident to me in this story is the father's initial reaction. His
son dissed him in the worst way possible, and what did the father do? *"And
so the father liquidated assets and divided them"* (Luke 15:12, The Voice). No
hesitation. No trying to dissuade his rebellious son, or even rebuke him for
treating him so terribly. He let the son go, freely.

Take a moment and think about that. The father truly loved his son.
We think that when you love someone, if they do something you deem
wrong, you must interject and stop them from making a huge mistake.
But this loving father allowed his son to do what he had already set his
mind to do. There was no controlling or fear motivation coming from the
father, just like with God. We have free will. That's how God created us.
Although it would be easier sometimes if He were to interject, He allows us
to choose. Every time!

God is a gentleman gently knocking on our heart's door, always pur-
suing us with His great love. Yet He will never bang the door down or make
us do something.

Of course, the story ends in an unfathomable way. As we read it, we're
waiting for the axe to fall, for the hammer to drop as the son slinks his way

home, head hanging in shame. But no! This story is about the father's amazing grace. What does he do? He sees the son coming and enfolds him in a loving embrace. Even then, he could start reprimanding his son, despite being excited to see him safe, but no. There was no shame attached, no guilt given, just a celebration that his son had returned. That is our beyond astonishing God—the good Father!

LOVING DADDY

When we hear the word "father," what comes to mind? For me, it brings up the picture of a stern man, one who is respected but also feared, as in children are slightly afraid of him. He is more concerned with how you behave and he tells you to be quiet when you're having too much fun. Life is serious with him around and the level of intimacy is a one out of ten at best.

Then there's the word "daddy." What does this word bring to mind? To me, it brings a sense of calm. I think of someone I can run up to and ask any question without fear. It brings about a confidence that I can do anything, because if I fall, my daddy will be there to pick me up.

See the difference? Maybe these words don't carry as much weight for you, but I feel the difference greatly. I am excited to call my heavenly Father "Daddy."

> If the Spirit of God is leading you, then take comfort in knowing you are His children. You see, you have not received a spirit that returns you to slavery, so you have nothing to fear. The Spirit you have received adopts you and welcomes you into God's own family. That's why we call out to Him, "Abba! Father!" as we would address a loving daddy.
> —Romans 8: 14–15 (The Voice, emphasis added)

This is the most relevant verse in my life right now. It gives me joy and puts a smile on my face every single time I read it.

When we say yes to God, we receive His Spirit, the same one that adopts us into that beautiful kingdom, gives us God's inheritance, and holds us close, like the loving Daddy He is!

LET'S PRAY

Thank You, Lord, that I get to call You my Daddy! My Abba Father! Thank You that You call me your daughter! I am so blessed to be a child of God, the God who doesn't look down on me in disappointment, but rather sees me as His precious child. I thank You that Your love for me is never-ending and unconditional. You are a good, good Father. Please remind me of that when I forget who I am. Who I am is Your daughter. Thank You, Jesus. May I walk around with that confidence and knowledge today in everything I do. Amen.

CHAPTER ELEVEN

OUR UNIQUE IDENTITY

There are different kinds of gifts, but the same Spirit distributes them.
—1 Corinthians 12:4 (NIV)

AS WE'VE DISCUSSED, KNOWING WHO WE ARE IS SO IMPORTANT. WE ARE the children of God! We are many other things, but the foundation on which we base our lives is knowing that there is a God who made us, loves us, is for us, and calls us His children.

We have a second identity as well, and that is our unique identity. You may be wondering, do we all just meld together at some point, as children of God? Are we supposed to all follow the same doctrine, do the same things that other Christians do, and be an obedient army to loose ourselves en masse? No, absolutely not.

Take a second and think about nature. When you look outside—let's say it's late spring—you see that the grass is starting to turn green, as are the other shrubs and bushes. But green isn't the only new color you see. Buds are sprouting on everything from the beautiful lilacs to the gorgeous blood-red rosebushes. There are blue jays singing, along with robins, excitedly awaiting the arrival of their new little ones. The water shifts as ice starts to melt and movement is seen below the surface once more. The rain comes, bringing dark clouds to wash away all the grime, and the sun peaks through to welcome a new day. Butterflies dance on the wind and gophers play. There is life, God-breathed life, and it is anything but ordinary or boring. It is anything but one solid bland color.

God is such an artist, and we see it so well in nature. So for us to think that He doesn't have a wonderful, creative gift placed inside us would be a little off the mark. We are all created to be loved by perfect love, which is God. And we are also created with a beautiful plan in mind. We carry something of great and unique value. The incredible thing is, it's different for each and every one of us. Even though you may have certain abilities that your parents had, too, there is something different about you. Even if you are a quadruplet, you have something irreplaceable to offer the world that's different from the other three people who look just like you. Even your fingerprints are different!

UNIQUE YET CONNECTED

We have something special to offer this world. God put something in you to share that will help increase what is good on the earth, yet when we call ourselves believers, we are connected to each other as well. The best illustration I've found of this comes from the Bible:

Just as a body is one whole made up of many different parts, and all the different parts comprise the one body, so it is with the Anointed One. We were all ceremonially washed through baptism together into one body by one Spirit. No matter our heritage—Jew or Greek, insider or outsider—no matter our status—oppressed or free—we were all given the one Spirit to drink. Here's what I mean: the body is not made of one large part but of many different parts. Would it seem right for the foot to cry, "I am not a hand, so I couldn't be part of this body"? Even if it did, it wouldn't be any less joined to the body. And what about an ear? If an ear started to whine, "I am not an eye; I shouldn't be attached to this body," in all its pouting, it is still part of the body. Imagine the entire body as an eye. How would a giant eye be able to hear? And if the entire body were an ear, how would an ear be able to smell? This is where God comes in. God has meticulously put this body together; He placed each part in the exact place to perform the exact function He wanted. If all members were a single part, where would the body be? So now, many members function within the one body. The eye cannot wail at the hand, "I have no need for you," nor could the head bellow at the feet, "I won't go one more step with you." It's actually the opposite. The members who seem to have the weaker functions are necessary to keep the body moving; the body parts that seem less important we treat as some of the most valuable; and those unfit, untamed, unpresentable members we treat with an even greater modesty. That's something the more presentable members don't need. But God designed the body in such a way that greater significance is given to the seemingly insignificant part. That way there should be no division in the body; instead, all the parts mutually depend on and care for one another. If one part is suffering, then all the members suffer alongside it. If one member is honored, then all the members celebrate alongside it. You are the body of the Anointed, the Liberating King; each and every one of you is a vital member.

—1 Corinthians 12:12-27 (The Voice)

As you can see, each of us is vital. Your part is needed! Your talent is important to create the whole picture. Even though you may not see the whole picture, you know the One who does.

Do you know what your unique identity is? Maybe you think you do, yet there is something more to be discovered.

FINDING YOUR UNIQUE IDENTITY

If you don't know what your special talent or ability is yet, that's okay. Finding it should be a joyful adventure. Even so, always start by going to God. Ask God what it is and for Him to reveal to you.

I also have a few questions that may get you on your way.

- What did you love to do as a child?
- What do you love doing now?
- What are you best qualities? What do you excel at?
- What are you doing when you feel most alive and free?
- What would you do for free, but end up getting paid for it?

These questions helped me when I didn't realize that I had a unique identity. There was a point in my life when I believed I was just here to do any old job. I didn't realize I could do something I enjoyed doing and that also helped others. When I realized I had something unique to offer, it was a good day for me. Today can be that day for you, too!

PRESSURE OFF

If you don't know what your unique identity is yet, but you have felt a lot of pressure to find out what it is, maybe from your parents or your spouse, I have good news. First of all, if you feel like you need to find out what your talent is, and soon, take some time to just be quiet with God. Once again, if you're acting out of a fear place, the decision will be no good. I would know! Make a decision in a place of rest and peace; if that isn't your home, find another place to go.

After about a year of selling cars at Toyota, my boss took me aside and asked me what was holding me back.

"What do you mean?" I asked.

"There's something holding you back. You don't seem to fully committed to selling cars."

Initially I was mad, because I thought he was calling me lazy. But then he did something pretty cool: he asked me to think about it, right then, in the middle of my workday. He was giving me permission to go think it over.

I got up and went to Starbucks with my binder—I love writing things out, especially when it comes to big life decisions. I wrote down a few questions for myself. As I sat there sipping my latte, I asked myself why I had started working at the dealership. I could have lied to myself and said that I was being ambitious, but the truth was that I had been operating out of a fear place. I wanted to make more money for my family, since my husband and I didn't think enough money was coming in.

I then asked myself another question: did I want to still be doing this in twenty years? Is this what I wanted my life to look like? The answer was a quick and surprising. No!

I realized I wasn't meant to be there anymore. Instant peace came over me as I made the decision to quit. In fact, I gave my two weeks' notice that day. It was one of the best decisions I ever made, as it came out of a secure place of being loved and knowing that money wasn't the most important thing. Raising two kids and gaining back my marriage were much more important to me.

Sometimes we get so busy living our so-called lives that we don't take the time to reflect, to really think about what we're doing and why. I'm giving you permission to take a reassessment coffee break right now and ask yourself some of these important questions. You're worth it!

The other beautiful thing is that, in the end, it doesn't really matter what you do but *how* you do it. That may sound like blasphemy, but hear me out.

WITHOUT LOVE

What if I speak in the most elegant languages of people or in the exotic languages of the heavenly messengers, but I live without love? Well then, anything I say is like the clanging of brass or a crashing cymbal. What if I have the gift of prophecy, am blessed with knowledge and insight to all the mysteries, or what if my faith is strong enough to scoop a mountain from its bedrock, yet I live without love? If so, I am nothing. I could give all that I have to feed the poor, I could surrender my body to be burned as a martyr, but if I do not live in love, I gain nothing by my selfless acts.

—1 Corinthians 13:1–3 (The Voice)

We can do amazing things in this life—save lives, give money to charity, help the needy and homeless—but if we don't have love, it's all useless. I know that is a bold statement, but let's flip it around for a second. If you don't have love, it means nothing. But if you do anything out of love, it means everything.

Let me repeat that. Whatever you do, if you do it out of a place of love, it matters! If you clean toilets for a living, and you do it with love, it matters. If you

> THE SMALLEST ACT, DONE IN LOVE, HAS A RESOUNDING IMPACT THAT ECHOES FOR ETERNITY.

shovel snow for a living, and you do it caring for the people you shovel snow for, it matters. The smallest act, done in love, has a resounding impact that echoes for eternity.

So for all you moms out there playing playdough, cleaning up toys, changing diapers, and kissing boo-boos, when you do it in love, it matters. Greatly!

Finding your unique identity is a fabulous adventure worth going on, but in the end, whatever you do, if it's done in love, you are making an impact on this earth.

Whatever you do, work at it with all your heart, as working for the Lord, not for human masters, since you know that you will receive an inheritance from the Lord as a reward. It is the Lord Christ you are serving.

—Colossians 3:23–24

You may be thinking, *I don't know that I can do anything in love, because I'm so mad all the time, or sad all the time. It's too hard to do things joyfully and with love in my life.* That's okay! Also, as I said earlier, we don't have to do anything in life alone. We have perfect love on our side, the God of the universe, and He will help us do anything and everything if we allow Him to. So allow Him to pour His incredible love into you so that it fills you to the brim with His love so that it has no option but to pour out into the rest of your life.

Whatever it is you do, do it with love and passion, enjoying this life that Jesus died to give you. It all matters because *you* matter.

LET'S PRAY

Lord, thank You that I am part of the body of Christ. Thank You that the people I see around me are part of that body, and even if I don't understand what is going on with the rest of the body, I can trust that we are one in You. Thank You that I carry a special and unique part of the body, and if I don't know exactly what that might be, I can trust that You have a plan. Thank You that I know that if I do something in love, it impacts this world and the body of Christ. Allow me to see others as being "in Christ" when I may otherwise feel frustrated. In this way, the world will know who You are, as we are one in You and You in us. Amen.

CHAPTER TWELVE

FAITH IS BIGGER THAN FEAR

"Don't be afraid because I am there with you."
—Genesis 26:24 (The Voice)

WE'VE TALKED ABOUT HOW WE ALL HAVE FEARS, EVEN THOUGH THERE
are many different kinds of fears. I've talked about real love, and how it
comes from God above and can dispel any fear. Now it's time to put my
money where my mouth is. Does it work? Does real love really take your
fear away? Can it change things? Can it make the impossible, possible?

Yes!

So often we fear what's to come or something we've made up in our
heads (like zombies), yet these things have not come to pass or are not
real. We can be free from these fears by focusing on what *is* real: God's never-ending love for us.

But what about when fears are real? Or when a situation is staring you
in the face that calls for some serious fear? What then?

Let me take you on the journeys of three people who had every right
to be very afraid, yet they were not.

DEN OF LIONS

You may have heard of Daniel, one of God's people in the Bible. Well, let
me give you a little backstory. Daniel, at a young age, was taken captive
along with many of his people and brought to a strange land by a strange
king named Nebuchadnezzar. The king decided to take the young, strong,
and brightest men of the land that he'd lain siege to and teach them the
language and literature of the Chaldeans, who lived in Babylonia.

Daniel was raised in a Hebrew home and had learned that there was only one true God. Even once he was taken captive and learned the ways of the Chaldeans, he never wavered from his childhood faith.

Quickly, Daniel gained favor with the king and was appointed governor over the whole province of Babylon. A few more great kings came and went, yet Daniel was able to remain in high standing with each new king.

He was a man of character. Seeing his good position with the new king, Darius, some of the other leaders, governors, and officers became terribly jealous. They devised a plan to get rid of Daniel.

The governors and officers agreed and went to the king with what they thought would be a way to entrap Daniel.

Conspirators *(to the king)*: *May King Darius live forever! All the leaders of the empire—the governors, prefects, officers, advisors, and other administrators—have consulted together and are in complete agreement that the king should issue an edict and enforce it strictly to the effect that anyone who prays to another—whether divine or human—except for you, of course, good king, for a period of 30 days, will be thrown into the lions' den. Now, O king, we ask that you establish such an ordinance and sign it into law, so that it cannot be changed. For the laws enacted by the Medes and Persians cannot be rescinded.*

After considering their proposal, King Darius signed the ordinance and made it law.

—Daniel 6:6–9 (The Voice)

Daniel was in the king's court and most certainly heard the news. He had always prayed to God in his home, three times per day. That was just part of his life, like breathing. He was very aware that his natural tendencies were now against the law, so he had a choice to make: stop publicly praying for a month to escape death, or continue on.

Let's find out what he decided.

Even though Daniel was aware the king had signed the ordinance into law, he continued to do what he always did. He would go home, ascend the stairs to the upper room—which had windows facing toward Jerusalem—and get down on his knees three times a day and pray to his God and praise Him.

—Daniel 6:10 (The Voice)

He made his decision and it was clear: Daniel put his faith and full trust in God. He had done the same up until this point, so why would this day be any different?

He made a courageous decision to do what he knew he needed to do, regardless of the law. Not an easy decision. Here in North America, when we break a law there is a fine, or jail time. Daniel faced something much worse: a lion's den. He very much took on the attitude and words King David had spoken long before: *"in God I trust and am not afraid. What can man do to me?"* (Psalm 56:11) Well, we are about to find out.

With his honor at stake, the king had no choice. He gave the order for Daniel to be captured. Before Daniel was thrown into the pit with the lions, the king spoke to him.

Darius: *May your God, the God you have served so faithfully, rescue you!*

Daniel was thrown into the lions' den and a stone was brought in and placed over the opening to shut the mouth of the den. The king himself sealed it with his own signet ring and with the signets of his nobles. That way no one could tamper with the pit and nothing could happen to change Daniel's fate.

—Daniel 6:16–17 (The Voice)

Have you ever been to the zoo? Gone on a safari? Have you seen a lion face to face?

I went to the zoo a year ago and stood at the big lion cage. I stared at the male lion for a while, thinking, *Wow! They really are huge! Their heads are about as big as from my waist to the top of my head. That thing could very easily kill me and eat me if it wanted to. They don't call a lion the king of the jungle for nothing.*

Needless to say, it was a lot bigger than I had thought. Even its paw was about the size of my head.

Lions are beautiful creatures, but they are also very intimidating. If I was thrown into a den full of lions, I can imagine the fear that would grip me. Daniel was thrown into a den filled with very large lions, and he had every human right to be terrified. The story could have ended there. Although if it did, we would probably not be reading about it so many years later.

As the king rushed to the den in the morning to see if by some miracle Daniel was still alive, a very interesting thing happened:

Daniel (*to the king*): *Long live the king! As soon as you shut the mouth of this den, My God sent His heavenly representative to shut the mouths of these hungry lions so that they could not hurt me. He has rescued me...*

—Daniel 6:21–22 (The Voice)

Wow! A miracle indeed. Part of me wonders, was Daniel at all afraid in the den? Did he have full peace and get sleep knowing that God had sent His messenger to close their mouths? Had he become so bold as to pet some of them, or did he just keep his distance? We don't know and I don't think it really matters, because long before the lion's den incident, Daniel made his decision to trust God. All the way to death.

How can someone who should be afraid not be? It's all about focus. Do we honestly believe that we can trust God? The answer is in our behavior. We always trust in something, and it shows in how we react to difficult situations.

You may be thinking, *I would love to trust God for big things, and I would like my faith to grow.* I thought the same a little while back, and when I didn't see results to my liking, I got very mad at myself. Why was I not trusting God more? It was made clear to me whilst reading *The Shack*:

"So why do I have so much fear in my life?" asked Mack.

"Because you don't believe. You don't know that we love you. The person who lives by their fears will not find freedom in my love. I am not talking about rational fears regarding legitimate dangers, but imagined fears, and especially the projection of those into the future. To the degree that those fears have a place in your life, you neither believe I am good nor know deep in your heart that I love you. You sing about it; you talk about it, but you don't know it," Jesus said.[34]

When we know that God truly loves us, trust is a byproduct. Think about it. Who is the person you trust most in this world? Why do you trust them, and do you feel loved by them? The amazing thing is that we don't have to strive to try and trust God more. The more we get to know Him and His incredible love, the more we automatically trust Him! Isn't that good news?

Daniel devoted three times a day to talking with God, conversing, praying, and getting to know Him more. It makes more sense now that Daniel would trust God so willingly.

BEATEN AND IMPRISONED

I'd like to tell you the story of a man named Paul, but first I need to give you some background. Stories of Paul can be found in the Book of Acts. Before he was Paul, though, he was Saul.

Jesus of Nazareth had just finished rocking the world with His presence. He performed many amazing miracles, healed the sick, fed the hungry, and clothed the poor. If this was all He had done, people would have left Him alone. But Jesus said that He was the Son of God, the Messiah, and *that* had most religious people of the day (the Pharisees) up in arms, to the point that they imprisoned Him, beat Him, and finally killed Him. Death couldn't keep Him, though, and on the third day after His death He was resurrected and showed Himself to many people, including His disciples.

Jesus did many more things after He was resurrected, and then He was lifted into Heaven. After this, Jesus's disciples start sharing the good news that Jesus was the living Son of God, the Messiah, the one true King. Many people became believers, but a lot of people were also very upset;

---

34 Wm. Paul Young, *The Shack* (Newbury Park, CA: Windblown Media, 2007), 142.

they believed that anyone following Jesus's teaching were evil and needed to be punished.

Saul was one of those angry people.

Back to Saul—this fuming, raging, hateful man who wanted to kill every last one of the Lord's disciples: he went to the high priest in Jerusalem for authorization to purge all the synagogues in Damascus of followers of the way of Jesus.

—Acts 9:1–2 (The Voice)

We can see that Saul in no way believed that Jesus was who He said He was. In fact, Saul wanted everyone who did believe this to die. Then he encountered the Lord—literally. A bright light appeared on the road Saul was travelling and a voice said, *"I am Jesus. I am the One you are attacking"* (Acts 9:5, The Voice).

A few other events followed, and needless to say, Saul became a believer and was referred to afterward as Paul, which means "humble." This is significant, as Saul was anything but humble. He was arrogant and believed he was right and all others were so wrong that he wanted them to die. This is truly an incredible turnaround for this man, so much so that the other disciples had a hard time believing Paul was genuine at first.

Paul, along with a few other disciples, then went far and wide preaching the gospel of Jesus as Lord of all. On their journey, they ended up in Philippi, a Roman city.

Paul cast out a demon from a slave girl, and it ended up being a really big deal. The owners of the slave were very upset.

The crowd joined in with insults and insinuations, prompting the city officials to strip them naked in the public square so they could be beaten with rods. They were flogged mercilessly and then were thrown into a prison cell. The jailer was ordered to keep them under the strictest supervision. The jailer complied, first restraining them in ankle chains, then locking them in the most secure cell in the center of the jail.

—Acts 16:22–24 (The Voice)

Imagine that you were doing nothing wrong, and in fact had just helped a slave girl into freedom. Then you're mercilessly beaten and imprisoned as though you had just brutally attacked and killed someone. Yikes. What would you be feeling at this time? I believe I would feel fear. Fear for the future, fear of dying in a cell, and some anger for being misjudged.

These men, though, coming from a time they had spent with the Holy Spirit, and feeling secure in who God said He was and who they were in Him, did something entirely different.

Picture this: It's midnight. In the darkness of their cell, Paul and Silas—after surviving the severe beating—aren't moaning and groaning; they're praying and singing hymns to God.

—Acts 16:25 (The Voice)

Wait, what? They almost died by being beaten, and now they were in shackles and imprisoned. Why did they feel no fear? How can that be? Humanly, this is not possible.

They had had a very real and personal encounter with the Most High and living God, and this is why. When fear should be present, they prayed and sang instead. Their focus was set on how powerful, loving, and amazing their God was, not on any of the circumstances around them. No matter what happened to them, they knew that God was with them. So they really and truly had nothing to fear.

What happens next is beyond incredible. It really makes the words of Mark 10:27 come to life (*"With man this is impossible, but not with God; all things are possible with God"*).

Suddenly the ground begins to shake, and the prison foundations begin to crack. You can hear the sound of jangling chains and the squeak of cell doors opening. Every prisoner realizes that his chains have come unfastened. The jailer wakes up and runs into the jail. His heart sinks as he sees the doors have all swung open. He is sure his prisoners have escaped, and he knows this will mean death for him, so he pulls out his sword to commit suicide. At that moment, Paul sees what is happening and shouts out at the top of his lungs,

Paul: *Wait, man! Don't harm yourself! We're all here! None of us has escaped.*

The jailer sends his assistants to get some torches and rushes into the cell of Paul and Silas. He falls on his knees before them, trembling. Then he brings them outside.

Jailer: *Gentlemen, please tell me, what must I do to be liberated?*

—Acts 16:26–30 (The Voice)

First God physically shook the foundation, freeing the disciples from jail. Even so, they didn't run away. They showed respect to the jailer in not letting him kill himself.

They could have left at that point, but the jailer asked them a very important question. You can practically hear the change in the jailer's voice as he calls them "gentlemen." He could have called them criminals, low-lifes, anything derogatory, yet he called them gentlemen, as they had just proven themselves to be. This jailer had physically bound them up, so they very well could have left him there crying, but just as they had been shown mercy from the living God, they showed him mercy, too.

Paul and Silas: *Just believe—believe in the ultimate King, Jesus, and not only will you be rescued, but your whole household will as well.*

The jailer brings them to his home, and they have a long conversation with the man and his family. Paul and Silas explain the message of Jesus to them all. The man washes their wounds and feeds them, then they baptize the man and his family. The night ends with Paul and Silas in the jailer's home, sharing a meal together, the whole family rejoicing that they have come to faith in God.

—Acts 16:31–34 (The Voice)

We see that Paul and Silas, with faith and security in the Most High God, could overcome fear when it was staring them right in the face. They even shared the gospel with the man who had imprisoned them. Incredible!

This actually reminds me of a strategy I use to overcome my fear of the dark. These men, in the dark, beaten and chained, prayed and sang praises to God. When I wake in the middle of the night and feel fear try to take over,

I sing a praise song in my head. Guess what? The fear, it's gone! You cannot sing praise songs to God, or even pray for someone else, and feel fear at the same time. You just cannot. Try it. I promise, God will never let you down if you give Him the opportunity to shine through you.

I also promise that on this journey of getting to know God, and discovering how much He truly loves you, your faith will automatically start to blossom before your very eyes. Just like these amazing men of faith—Daniel, Paul, and Silas. Then, as you grow in your relationship with God and circumstances arise, faith will replace the fear.

> I PROMISE THAT ON THIS JOURNEY OF GETTING TO KNOW GOD, AND DISCOVERING HOW MUCH HE TRULY LOVES YOU, YOUR FAITH WILL AUTOMATICALLY START TO BLOSSOM BEFORE YOUR VERY EYES.

LET'S PRAY

Lord Jesus, thank You for always being with me, just like You were with Daniel in the lions' den, and also with Paul and Silas in their prison cell. You gave them a way out because their focus was on You.

Lord, I want my focus to be on You and Your goodness, and I thank You for Your patience with me in this learning curve. You are so good, and worthy to be praised! I want to know You more and I thank You that as our relationship grows, my faith will automatically grow, too.

Show me today, specifically, how much You love me, and guide me to show others Your love as well. Thank You that Your perfect love casts out all fear. Remind me of this today when I feel that fear creeping up, that it has no place in my life where You are concerned, and I know that You care for every part of me. Thank You! In Jesus's name, amen.

CHAPTER THIRTEEN

DO YOU THINK LIONS WALK AROUND AFRAID?

The wicked flee though no one pursues, but the righteous are as bold
as a lion.

—Proverbs 28:1 (emphasis added)

THERE'S A GOOD REASON THAT THE LORD IS REFERRED TO AS A LION
many times in the Bible. Have you ever watched a lion? Studied up on
them? I already wrote a little about lions during the section about Daniel,
but there's more. They are fierce, fearless, unafraid, and strong. Every action
they do, they do it with confidence.

Lions live in the wild, where anything can happen. And yet a lion
sleeps anywhere from eighteen to twenty hours a day. Where do they
sleep? Up in a tree, for protection? In a cave? Nope. They usually sleep under a tree for shade from the hot sun, or right out in the open. When they
lay down their head to rest, that's exactly what they do—rest. They don't
keep one eye open, ever ready for an attack. They simply rest.

Do you think lions walk around afraid? The obvious answer is no.
They walk around with a confident stride, knowing who they are—and
they own it.

From day to day, how do you walk around? When I don't remember
who I am in Christ, I can easily let the world happen to me. I take on a de-
fensive stance instead of an active stance. I let emotions run me, instead of
enjoying them, and I let fear walk all over me. Maybe that's just me.

But there's so much more to this, so let's delve deeper.

WHO IS GOD?

Nine times out of ten, I think, we underestimate our God—His greatness, His faithfulness, and His unconditional love. This is not a reprimand, but a reminder of who we serve.

Isaiah 40 states the grandeur of God. It's not just some simple idea to put a warm fuzzy feeling in us once in a while.

Face it; the nations are nothing but a drop in the bucket, only a smidgen on the scales by the reckoning of God. He can pick up entire islands as if they are grains of dirt ... Don't you know, haven't you heard or even been told from your earliest memories how the earth came to be? Who else could have done it except God, enthroned high above the earth? ... The Holy One asks, "Do you really think you can find someone or something to compare to Me? My equal?" Look at the myriad of stars and constellations above you. Who set them to burning, each in its place? Who knows those countless lights each by name? They obediently shine, each in its place, because God has the great strength and strong power to make it so.
—Isaiah 40:15, 21–22, 25–26 (The Voice)

He created everything we see—the world around us, the stars, the entire universe. Our God truly is mighty! He also made you and me. Maybe, just maybe, it's time we started believing it.

Our Lord is great. Nothing is impossible with His overwhelming power. He is loving, compassionate, and wise beyond all measure.
—Psalm 147:5 (The Voice)

Even when we get to heaven, I don't think we will know everything about God. He is so much more amazing, incredible, and worthy of praise than I can give Him credit for. But this is also a great thing, because if you could gain all the knowledge there is to know about God, what kind of God would He be? Not much of one, in my opinion. He cannot be fully figured out.

This is a part of my walk with God that I absolutely love: no matter how much I know about God, and continually find out, there is always more. It keeps me in constant anticipation about knowing more and going even deeper with the God of the universe. No matter how much I think I know about how much He loves me, there is *way* more. That is good news! God has done incredible miracles, and a lot of them are documented in the Bible, and even today. Though we could go through a few right now, I believe I'll leave the excitement of reading about it in the Bible to you. When you do, you'll be unlocking the treasures of His greatness. Let God speak to you personally through each of the stories proclaiming His goodness.

I encourage you to ask God, while you're reading His word, for Him to make it real to you, and for Him to speak to you through it. When you do, it's like reading the Bible for the first time. At least, it was for me.

INTRICATELY MADE

I always loved biology as a teenager. I found it fascinating to learn all about the human body and the amazing creation that it is. If you don't quite recall the details, let me refresh your memory.

Think about what you went through before you were born. You were created by two cells: an egg and a sperm. After three weeks, you have a heart *and* it's beating. You continue to grow, forming everything from your future teeth to toenails. Then, when you are fully formed (usually), you are squeezed—and yes, I mean squeezed—through a very small opening, all the while not breathing. Your head has to contort to fit through that small opening. Anyone who was naturally born had this happen to them. We go from living in fluid one second to needing air the next. This has always blown me away.

Then take a moment and think about your body and the normal, everyday functions it performs. Your heart pumps all your blood around your body three times a minute. You also have sixty thousand miles of blood vessels inside your body,[35] enough to circumnavigate the Earth twice. Last

---

35 *Everyday Health,* "10 Amazing Facts About Your Blood Vessels." July 20, 2015 (http://www.everydayhealth.com/news/10-amazing-facts-about-your-blood-vessels/).

one. Your body produces twenty-five million new cells every second. Every thirteen seconds, you produce more cells than there are people in the United States.

Our bodies truly are incredible—far greater than we often give it credit for. In fact, a lot of us wake up on a regular basis feeling like nothing is amazing in this world. Even more common, we wake up feeling awful about ourselves, carrying no worth or value, which leads very quickly to depression.

Wake up! You are an intricate being made to perfection by a loving and powerful Heavenly Father who literally would do anything for you. Do you even realize how wonderful you are? Let's start to realize who we are and our incredible worth through our Creator. Then we can change this beautiful blue and green ball we live on.

We've just started on a path to finding out how amazing and powerful our God truly is, and now you can see just how great you are. Put those two together and what do you have? An unstoppable force.

When we believe that God is who He says He is, He comes and lives inside us—not just spiritually but physically.

But you do know the Spirit because He lives with you, and He will dwell in you.
—John 14:17 (The Voice)

Wait! This almighty, powerful, living God lives inside us?

Remember that God has established our relationship with you in the Anointed One, and He has anointed and commissioned us for this special mission. He has marked us with His seal and placed His Spirit in our hearts as a guarantee, a down payment of the things to come.
—2 Corinthians 1:21–22 (The Voice)

When we believe that God is who He says He is, that He placed His Spirit in us as a guarantee, look out!

The devil wins when we don't see our potential in Christ. We say, "Well, I'm *just* a teenager. I'm *just* a construction worker. I'm *just* a stay-at-home mom. I'm *just* a sinner. I'm *just* a human being." These are only a few of the lies we believe day to day instead of waking up and thanking God for giving us a new day, realizing that as we walk with God throughout the day, nothing is too big for Him to conquer and overcome. Which makes us overcomers! We can more than just survive, we can thrive.

Inspirational writer and author Holly Gerth says,

> If you really take hold of who you are and what you're called to do, there will be NO stopping you. That's because there is no stopping Him in you—and He's got bigger plans for your life than you've ever imagined![36]

Today, ask God to show you a little more of His amazing power at work in you, and to reveal more of His will for your life. Incredible things begin to happen when we ask.

SALVATION IS JUST THE BEGINNING

Many people believe that the big prize is getting saved. I agree that salvation is *huge*, and I am so thankful for my salvation through Jesus Christ. I'm so very excited to meet Him face to face one day. But being saved is just the beginning.

For the people who believe it is the big prize, what happens after? That's a boring, oatmeal kind of a life if you ask me. But just like Jesus said, *"I have come that they may have life, and have it to the full!"* (John 10:10). This isn't just a life where our greatest achievement is becoming saved and then trying not to screw up so we can get to

> THROUGH HIS POWER, WE ARE WORLD-CHANG-ERS AND DIFFER-ENCE-MAKERS. WITHOUT HIM, WE JUST FLOAT BY UNTIL THIS CANDLE OF OURS FLICKERS OUT.

---

36 Holly Gerth, *You're Already Amazing* (Grand Rapids, MI. Baker Publishing Group, 2012) 12.

heaven. No. It's a life where every day is a new and exciting opportunity to see what God can show you and do through you.

Through His power, we are world-changers and difference-makers. Without Him, we just float by until this candle of ours flickers out. We don't need Jesus just once to save our souls and then never need Him again. We need God every second of every day, in the good times and the bad. He promised to never leave us, so the choice lies with us. We can either ask Him to join us in our daily lives or strive in our own strength. I know through personal experience that doing life with God is way better than doing it without Him. Why don't I just walk daily with Him then? Well, I am human, but thankfully I have found the grace to laugh at myself when I try it on my own, instead of beating myself up over it.

So what are some things we may be able to do with God living inside of us?

> But those who trust in the Eternal One will regain their strength. They will soar on wings as eagles. They will run—never winded, never weary. They will walk—never tired, never faint.
>
> —Isaiah 40:31 (The Voice)

I love this promise, and it is absolutely one to meditate on. What did the prophet really mean when he said this? When we trust in God, we can do truly amazing things. He starts off big, too, with being able to fly! I love the idea of being able to fly. Maybe that's why I went skydiving. That experience was the closest I've felt to actually flying, on the way down with the chute open and just gliding slowing toward the earth, seeing way more than usual but still at a pace that you can breathe in all that is happening around you.

What's interesting in this passage from Isaiah is that flying, especially back then, was unheard of. So he tamed it down. Soar on wings like eagles! Too fantastical for you? Okay, then you will be able to run and not grow weary. Still too far-fetched? Then let's take it to a level where anyone with legs can understand. You will be able to walk and never get tired or faint!

That is truly how our faith works. God always meets us at our level, because He is so awesome like that. Are you at walking level? No problem.

Give your walking level of trust to God and you'll be able to walk forever. Feeling ready to run, or even fly? God's got your back! You will be able to soar on wings like eagles. I don't know about you, but I like the sound of that.

> *My children, you have come from God and have conquered these spirits because the One who lives within you is greater than the one in this world.*
>
> —1 John 4:4 (The Voice)

In our darkest moments, in the hardest parts of our lives, this verse provides a real reminder that the One who lives in us is in every way greater than anything around us. Does this mean life is easy as a believer? Sorry to disappoint you, but no. This world is at times cruel and unusual, but when we walk through the cruel and unusual, we do it joined with the most powerful force in all of the universe. The lion of Judah lives within us and walks along all paths with us.

Whenever I have a fear, I picture God as a huge lion standing right beside me, roaring that fear away—and that fear *has* to leave. Try it for yourself.

Ever seen the movie or read the book, *The Lion, the Witch, and the Wardrobe*? It's no wonder C.S. Lewis used the metaphor of God as a powerful lion.

BOLD AS A LION

When we rely on our own strength to carry us through the day-to-day stuff, fear attacks us when we're unaware of it. We worry and flee from monsters that we make up in our heads. Then, when the heavy stuff comes and we try to get through in our own strength, we often run away to something else to get our minds off it. This can be anything from alcohol, shopping, watching TV, drugs, or any other vices.

Does this make us weak? No, it makes us human. But thank the Lord we can rise above this, as we have the heavyweight champion of the world in our corner.

When we know He's in our corner, or simply remind ourselves, we truly can be as bold as lions. Remember all the things a lion does. It walks around with confidence and it sleeps peacefully, out in the open and easily. A lion fears no thing around it but walks with its head held high. It is not ashamed of being a lion; no, the lion wears its mane proud as king of the jungle. That's who we are with the King of the universe living inside of us.

Do whatever you need to do to remind yourself of this fact every single day. Then watch how quickly your life takes on a new beauty of its own, one you never knew was possible. As God very clearly asked me, and is now asking you, "Do you really think this is all I have for you?"

According to Romans 8:11, the same power that raised Christ from the dead is inside of you. Reread that and think about it for a second. God not only loves you more than you could ever imagine, but He also put inside you the power that raised Christ.

The power that raised Christ from the grave, the same power that lives in you, is there for every part of your life. It's there helping you forgive someone who hurt you beyond measure. It's there when you've lost someone close to you. It's there when you make snowmen with your children. It's not just there for the big stuff, because God cares about every single part of your life.

If you've read the Bible, you know some of the life-altering miracles and wonders God has done—like feeding five thousand people with just two loaves of bread and five fish. Jesus walked on water and turned water into wine, and God's power parted the Red Sea! He forgave sins, freed the captives, opened prison doors, and raised people from the dead. Incredible things happened in the Bible, but there's even better news:

> *I tell you the truth: whoever believes in Me will be able to do what I have done, but they will do even greater things, because I will return to be with the Father.*
>
> —John 14:12 (The Voice)

We can do even greater things when we have God living in us. I know that may be hard to believe, or you may not believe it at all, but He is speaking the truth. What are these greater things? They are different for every single person out there, including you.

LIFE AS A JUNGLE GYM

For my last birthday, I wanted to do something fun and daring. I decided to go to a place called Adrenaline Adventures. They have a fifty-foot jungle gym on which you can climb and go through obstacles until you reach the top and zip-line down. My brother and I had a blast.

It got me thinking, though. Life is kind of like this jungle gym. The people who believe the best moment is being saved are the people on the ground. They're comfortable to just stay there. But there is so much more. You start climbing up the steep wall, and halfway up, when you feel your muscles start to shake and fingers tremble, you wonder if you'll make it. Then you look up and see that it's only a little farther. You make it to the top of the first phase and feel a sense of wonder at what you've accomplished, feeling confident to move on to the next phase. You have a harness that's connected with two carabineers. Every time you get to a new phase, you disconnect the one carabineer and connect it to the next line. The main line runs through the whole jungle gym, connected to poles which run ten feet into the ground to keep them steady and unchanging. Even once you've disconnected the first carabineer, your second is still attached to a different line. You're always connected to the main line so that if you fall, one if not both lines will catch you.

The same goes in life. God is our main line; we simply need to remember that we are always connected to Him. He never, ever lets us go. And when we reach the next station and see that we have to jump onto a swinging tire and our feet have to leave the ledge, we can either be overcome with fear and stay where we are or remember that we're connected to the main line and that we have nothing to fear. Even if we drop, He will catch us.

When I was on the top level of this jungle gym and had to jump onto a knee board strung up in the air from a swinging tire I was clinging to, I was afraid. Not gonna lie. But I had to get down somehow and I knew the best way was to continue on. I also had my brother's voice cheering me on, my husband cheering me on from the ground, and the knowledge that I was connected to the main line. I was not going to plummet to my death. No, I would drop about three feet and hang there, safely.

I had a choice to make: let fear rule or faith rule.

Well, seeing as I am down on the ground now, continuing to live my life, you know which choice I made.

But the same is true with the big leaps we make in life. Ask yourself, are you connected to the main line? If so, then feel free to jump and know that when you put your trust in God, you will not only make the leap but soar on wings like eagles!

I can say from experience that the more leaps we make, the more confident we will be to do it again. You may start off jumping over a "puddle" in your life, but it'll be the gateway to the next amazing phase in your life. Take a moment, celebrate your victory, and then continue on.

Oh, and by the way, having people in your corner also helps. If you're not connected to people who lift you up and inspire you, make it a priority to find some. They are out there. Pray for God to put someone in your path. If you already have someone who is a source of encouragement, then thank God for that gift.

LET'S PRAY

Dear sweet Heavenly Father, thank You for dying in my place. I want to sincerely thank You for giving me the same power that raised Jesus back to life. I don't quite know what that means right now, but I'm so excited for You to show me amazing things.

I give my life to You, every part of it, and thank You that You want all of it—the good, the bad, the ugly, the small, the big, and everything in between! I know that when I trust You, I regain my strength and can soar on wings like eagles. Show me how to fly with You today!

I pray for abundant blessings in my life. Thank You for all the incredible promises You have for me! You are so good and worthy to be praised, and You gave me incredible authority over all the fear in my life. So right now I pray that You would show me in a real that I don't have to let fear rule my life in any way. Because I believe in You, I truly can walk around wherever I go, bold as a lion! In Jesus's name, amen.

CHAPTER FOURTEEN

LIFE WITHOUT FEAR

When Jesus spoke again to the people, he said, "I am the light of the world. Whoever follows me will never walk in darkness, but will have the light of life."

—John 8:12

LIFE WITHOUT FEAR. IS IT POSSIBLE? THAT'S THE QUESTION. YOU'VE reached the end of this book, and hopefully you weren't looking for a mathematical equation to magically lift all the fear out of your life. That's not how life is intended to be. Life is messy and dynamic. It's ever-moving and always changing, whether you like it or not.

I myself have not reached a place of never being afraid. Do I believe it's possible? Without God, not a chance. With God? I believe we can get pretty close, and thankfully God has given me examples of men and women who have stood in the face of fear, stared down the barrel of the gun, and had no fear whatsoever. Even so, I believe life is a journey on which we can either try to stay the same or constantly press forward, learn more, and grow.

As I have set out on this journey to know God and His love more, I can absolutely say that my fear has diminished more and more. Even when it does rear its ugly head, I run to God quicker. How can I do that? Because, in all honesty, it's not me! Simply being loved allows you to trust the One who loves you—and no one on this planet will ever love you more than God.

CROSSROADS

We now have a decision to make. Do we want to stay in this place of hiding from our fears, where we believe we will be safer and yet stay bound by invisible chains? Do we want to stay in our comfort zone of believing we have everything under our control? Do we want to try to fight our own fears and our own battles with the little strength we have left at the end of the day? Or do we want to realize that there's someone out there who is so much bigger than we are? He isn't far away and judgmental; He's the One who made you, loves you, and will provide a way for you every time you ask Him. Do we want to face our fears and push past our comfort zone with the God of the universe living inside us? Do we want to experience the freedom that brings? Do we want to live in the unknown, taking risks, and not experience fear because we know the One who does know?

Is this an easy journey? Nope. Who said anything about easy? Is this a worthwhile journey! Yes, yes, and yes again. Now's the time to decide. But here's the cool thing: whatever you decide, God is patiently waiting, always wanting the best for you, and never giving up on you. I know this for a fact.

A few years ago, I read *The Shack*. Afterward, I felt so close to God. I talked to Him all the time, not out of a guilty obligation out of a sweet excitement to see what He had to say about any given situation. I could feel a sweet union forming between us.

I wish that I could say it's only gotten stronger since then, but I'm human. After about a year of this, I talked to God less, and then I felt guilt about it—which, remember, is not God. I had to fight to get that relationship back. It's not that I ever stopped believing in God, or shunned Him, but He became a kind of afterthought.

We are human and will reach mountaintops, and also walk through low valleys. But even when we change, our God does not. His love *never* fails.

WALKING WITH US

If you were to walk down a dark alley this evening, alone, going home from some event, what sort of thoughts would pass through your mind? Would you be afraid? I know I would, naturally.

Now, let's say that I'm walking down that same dark alley, but instead of being alone, I have a linebacker walking me to the end. The biggest linebacker in history. And the catch is that I know he is for me, and if anything happens, if someone were to jump out with a gun or knife and try to hurt me, that linebacker would do everything in his power to protect me. Then I would walk down that dark alley with confidence.

The awesome thing is that we do have the biggest linebacker on our side. In any situation when we get afraid and feel afraid, all we have to do is remember that our God is with us through it all.

> *As I was with Moses, so I will be with you; I will never leave you nor forsake you.*
>
> —Joshua 1:5

> *When you pass through the waters, I will be with you.*
>
> —Isaiah 43:2

We're so often afraid of doing things alone, or being left behind, but the truth is that we are never alone. God's promise is that He will be with us.

When we face any fear, whether it's swimming, finding a husband or wife, killing a spider, or walking through a dark alley, we are not alone. We have the linebacker, the roaring lion of Judah, on our side. He is walking with us, ready to devour anything that comes against us, even if it's just the fear in our minds.

That's why we truly have nothing to fear.

REMEMBERING

Fear is a part of living. Fear is a force that will always come back to us and try to control our lives, every day most likely. But what's important is how fast we react to it, and what our reaction is. We don't have control over when fear will rear its ugly head. Maybe it's in the morning or in the middle of the afternoon, or in the middle of your first dinner with your future in-laws. We have no control over that.

What we do have control over is our reaction, how quick we remember that the linebacker, is right beside us. The first time your usual fear comes up, you may let it take you, but now you're aware of it. That's a great first step. Then, the next time it happens, you may remember that God is with you an hour after the fear hits. The next time, you may remember half an hour after the fear hits. Then you may remember ten minutes after, then five minutes, then one minute… until you get a fear attack and *immediately* counteract it with a bold statement: "No! The God of the universe is with me right now and I have nothing to fear! You have no control over me!" Remembering the truth is up to us!

Will we be ever rid of fear? No, it will always pursue us, but we can combat it quicker and quicker to the point that we barely feel its attack, with Christ's power living inside of us. Perfect love drives out fear!

HIS PROMISE

The verse of this book, which has been a constant, comes from 1 John 4:18:

> *There is no fear in love. But perfect love drives out all fear, because fear has to do with punishment. The one who fears is not made perfect in love.*

So when we press into that perfect love, which we know can come from no man, but God alone, it has to drive fear away. But what is in that perfect love? What is life like when we get to know that perfect love more and more?

> *The Holy Spirit produces a different kind of fruit: unconditional love, joy, peace, patience, kindheartedness, goodness, faithfulness, gentleness, and self-control.*
> —Galatians 5:22–23 (The Voice)

We cannot hide what we believe. What we believe, whether it's that pigs can fly or that the boogeyman lives in our closet, comes through in the fruit we produce. What's the fruit we produce? Anything you do or create is based out of your beliefs. So when we let fear rule, it shows. When we let love rule, it shows.

When we press into God's love, we automatically start producing things with more love; we have more joy, peace, and patience in our lives. This is God's promise to us.

If this sounds like a life worth living, something you want to know more about, you can make a declaration to God and yourself right now. What is it that you are most afraid of these days? Take a moment and think about it. If you're sick of feeling fear and letting it control your life, give it to God!

Lord, right now I am struggling with the fear of _____ _____. I'm beginning to understand how much You truly love me, and that gives me the freedom to trust You with this part of my life. I pray right now that _____ has no power in my life except that which I give it.

I want to give You all the power and glory in my life. I pray that this fear has no place in my life and that You, Lord, take this away right now, in Jesus's name. If it comes up again, Lord, please remind me of Your amazing power and grace over this situation.

Thank You that my life is changing right now for the better. I know that as You help me overcome this, I will have more strength and faith than before to continue on this path, to overcome the next obstacle with more peace and ease than ever before!

Please continue to mold me and show me other lies I may believe that have no place in my life. I love You, Lord, and thank You for loving me and knowing my name! Amen!

A NEW BEGINNING

May this be just the beginning of a beautiful new season in your life. I'm excited to see what God has in store for me, and even more excited to see what God has in store for you!

May you be blessed by the Lord, the Maker of heaven and earth.
—Psalm 115:15

Contact the Author
for Speaking Engagements

Learn more about Sylvia St.Cyr by checking out her blog at
www.sylviasblog.com

And by emailing
authorsylviastcyr@gmail.com

You can also follow her on social media at

Facebook: **www.facebook.com/authorsylviastcyr**
Twitter: **@Sylvia_StCyr**

www.ingramcontent.com/pod-product-compliance
Lightning Source LLC
LaVergne TN
LVHW051414080426
835508LV00022B/3085